The Complete Guide to

Working for Yourself

Everything the Self-Employed Need to Know About Taxes, Recordkeeping, and Other Laws

With Companion CD-ROM

By Beth Williams & Dr. Jean Murray

THE COMPLETE GUIDE TO WORKING FOR YOURSELF: EVERYTHING THE SELF-EMPLOYED NEED TO KNOW ABOUT TAXES, RECORDKEEPING, AND OTHER LAWS — WITH COMPANION CD-ROM

Copyright © 2008 by Atlantic Publishing Group, Inc.
1405 SW 6th Ave. • Ocala, Florida 34471 • 800-814-1132 • 352-622-1875–Fax
Web site: www.atlantic-pub.com • E-mail: sales@atlantic-pub.com
SAN Number: 268-1250

ISBN-13: 978-1-60138-048-7   ISBN-10: 1-60138-048-8

Library of Congress Cataloging-in-Publication Data

Williams, Beth, 1973-
  The complete guide to working for yourself : everything the
self-employed need to know about taxes, recordkeeping, and other
laws-with companion CD-ROM / by Beth Williams and Jean Wilson Murray.
      p. cm.
  Includes bibliographical references and index.
  ISBN-13: 978-1-60138-048-7
  ISBN-10: 1-60138-048-8
  1. Self-employed. 2. New business enterprises--Management. 3. Small
business--Management. I. Murray, Jean Wilson. II. Title.

  HD8036.W553 2008
  658'.041--dc22
                        2007049099

Printed on Recycled Paper

INTERIOR LAYOUT DESIGN: Vickie Taylor • vtaylor@atlantic-pub.com

Printed in the United States

We recently lost our beloved pet "Bear," who was not only our best and dearest friend but also the "Vice President of Sunshine" here at Atlantic Publishing. He did not receive a salary but worked tirelessly 24 hours a day to please his parents. Bear was a rescue dog who turned around and showered me, my wife Sherri, his grandparents Jean, Bob, and Nancy, and every person and animal he met (maybe not rabbits) with friendship and love. He made a lot of people smile every day.

We wanted you to know that a portion of the profits of this book will be donated to the Humane Society of the United States.

–Douglas & Sherri Brown

THE HUMANE SOCIETY
OF THE UNITED STATES©

The human-animal bond is as old as human history. We cherish our animal companions for their unconditional affection and acceptance. We feel a thrill when we glimpse wild creatures in their natural habitat or in our own backyard.

Unfortunately, the human-animal bond has at times been weakened. Humans have exploited some animal species to the point of extinction.

The Humane Society of the United States (HSUS) makes a difference in the lives of animals here at home and worldwide. The HSUS is dedicated to creating a world where our relationship with animals is guided by compassion. We seek a truly humane society in which animals are respected for their intrinsic value and where the human-animal bond is strong.

Want to help animals? We have plenty of suggestions. Adopt a pet from a local shelter or join the Humane Society and be a part of our work to help companion animals and wildlife. You will be funding our educational, legislative, investigative, and outreach projects in the United States and across the globe.

Or perhaps you'd like to make a memorial donation in honor of a pet, friend, or relative. You can through our Kindred Spirits program. And if you'd like to contribute in a more structured way, our Planned Giving Office has suggestions about estate planning, annuities, and even gifts of stock that avoid capital gains taxes.

Maybe you have land that you would like to preserve as a lasting habitat for wildlife. Our Wildlife Land Trust can help you. Perhaps the land you want to share is a backyard—that's enough. Our Urban Wildlife Sanctuary Program will show you how to create a habitat for your wild neighbors.

So you see, it's easy to help animals. And the HSUS is here to help.

The Humane Society of the United States
2100 L Street NW
Washington, D.C. 20037
202-452-1100
www.hsus.org

contents C

Chapter 3: Naming Your Business and Writing Your Business Plan 73

Chapter 7: Setting Your Price and Collecting Money 167

Chapter 8: Ways to Market Your Product or Service.................................. 187

Chapter 9: All About Self-Employed Taxes 205

Chapter 10: Easy Recordkeeping and Accounting 215

Chapter 11: Writing and Using Client Agreements.. 235

Chapter 12: Copyrights, Patents, and Trade Secrets... 241

foreword f

By Dr. Larina Kase

You dream of owning your own business. You dream of the day with no bosses or managers looking over your shoulder. You dream of the flexibility and freedom that you would have as a business owner. You dream of doing what you believe in and are great at every single day.

Despite your excitement at the prospect of owning your own business, you are stuck in dreamland. You have not taken action to turn it into reality.

Why is this?

For many people, perhaps the vast majority, I believe that the problem is simple: You do not know what to do. You do not know how to set up your company, register your company name, and file your taxes. These unknowns can become overwhelming and keep you from taking the plunge and building a successful company.

I am thrilled that you are reading *The Complete Guide to Working for Yourself* because it will solve those problems for you. If you have what it takes to be a business owner — vision, guts, determination, passion — then I do not want the unknowns to hold you back. The answers are here at your finger tips. These are answers that I wish I had when I started my business. They would have saved me a whole lot of time, energy, confusion, and stress. I learned the hard way, but you do not have to.

Beth Williams and Dr. Jean Murray take you by the hand and walk you through each step of the process. They take the time to address key issues that keep many people from working for themselves, such as insurance, retirement, and taxes.

You will learn how to write an effective business plan that will be the key to your company's success. Williams and Dr. Murray walk you through each part of the business plan so you know exactly what to include so that you can run your business professionally and efficiently. The accompanying CD-ROM contains sample business plans that you can easily alter to fit your business needs.

Once you set up your business, you need to market it to get customers or clients. Williams and Dr. Murray walk you through networking with other businesses and professionals, writing press releases, where to advertise, how to do promotions, and how to use the Internet to your advantage.

And you will need to run your business. You will learn how to be an effective manager and leader. *The Complete Guide to Working for Yourself* includes helpful tips and suggestions on hiring, handling, and firing your employees, so that you can make the most out of your business.

Starting your own business is a lot of hard work, but it is definitely worth it. You experience a feeling of accomplishment and pride that is like no other. Now that you have this book, you will not get stuck at the unknowns. Instead, you will sail through the fundamental decisions and create a business reality that feels like a dream.

About Dr. Larina Kase

Larina Kase PsyD, MBA is a business coach who helps entrepreneurs accomplish more than they ever thought possible. She specializes in the psychology of marketing, creating joint venture partnerships, and achieving expert status. Find her ideas in magazines such as Entrepreneur *and* Inc. *and get dozens of business-building resources at* **http://www.pascoaching.com.**

introduction

Many people dream of one day breaking free from the normal, nine-to-five world and starting their own businesses. Unfortunately, starting a small business is, for most of those people, merely a dream. The reality of starting and running a small business is hard work, and most businesses do not become a success overnight. Rather, it takes years of work and commitment to build a successful business.

Self-employment is the path many choose. You have likely heard the varying terms for self-employment, among them *freelancer*, *consultant*, *independent contractor*, and even *entrepreneur*.

According to the U.S. Census Bureau, there were 18.6 million small businesses with no employees in the United States in 2003, making up 70 percent of all U.S. businesses. Receipts from these small businesses totaled $830 million. So you are in good company if you want to be self-employed.

The Complete Guide to Working for Yourself: Everything the Self-Employed Need to Know About Taxes, Recordkeeping, and Other Laws is a valuable resource guide that will tell you what you need to know about the laws and taxes that apply to you as a small-business owner. It is a must read for anyone who has started, or has thought about starting, his or her own business.

You will also learn everything you need to know about legally organizing your business, hiring employees, and drafting contracts to use with clients and others, such as independent contractors. Just as important, you will learn the risks you should be aware of and how to legally protect yourself to ensure you have a long, successful business.

Take advantage of the companion CD-ROM, which includes legal forms, agreements, and contracts you can use as needed. You can also adjust the forms to suit your purposes. The key to your success as an entrepreneur is to educate yourself. Remember, education is an ongoing process, one that does not end when you are successful.

chapter 1

All About Working for Yourself

Many people would love to say that they work for themselves. Working for oneself can, indeed, be an exhilarating experience. But the one thing most people do not anticipate is the hard work and the long hours they have to put in, especially in the beginning.

You must understand the level of work involved in being self-employed before you take the plunge. And it is absolutely essential that you view your business as just that: a business. One of the reasons people fail in self-employment is that they fail to look at their job as a real business. Leaving your job for the self-employed life means you are going to have to take on responsibilities you have probably never had before. For example, in a regular job, your employer takes care of things like employee taxes. When you are self-employed, however, you will have to pay your own federal, state, and local taxes on a regular schedule set by the government. If you fail to pay your taxes, you will face fines and other penalties.

You must educate yourself as to your responsibilities as a self-employed individual. If you fail to do so, you will run into far too many headaches, and you most likely will not make it far in self-employment. Take the time now to learn about small-business laws and taxes, and you will save precious time and money in the future.

The Good – Advantages of Working for Yourself

There are numerous advantages to working for yourself. People who work for themselves generally do something they love, something about which they are passionate. Because you love what you are doing you likely are going to be even more motivated to make your business successful.

One of the most alluring benefits of self-employment is the fact that you can conceivably make as much money as you want. It all boils down to your motivation to work hard and reach your goals, one of which is likely to bring you more money working for yourself than you made when you were working for someone else.

You may not make as much or more than you did at your regular job in the beginning. Of course, that is not a hard and fast rule. Some self-employed people do make a lot of money right from the start, but you should be aware that it may very well take you months or even years to make the amount of money you want each year. But, if you are committed and you work hard, you will likely reach success and make the money you want. To that end, always make sure you keep accurate records of the money you are making and the money you are spending.

When you work for yourself, you also have the advantage of determining how much clients will pay you for your services. For example, let us say you are a public relations specialist with several years of experience. If you worked for a public relations firm, you might earn $20 an hour, which is not a bad hourly rate. However, if you are a freelance public relations specialist, you can charge upwards of $75 an hour, and you will find companies willing to pay that rate.

In addition to deciding what to charge, you are not beholden to a corporation. You cannot be fired in the traditional sense of the word. Of course, a client can decide to stop working with you and vice versa. You have the power to decide which projects you will accept. In the beginning, you may feel as though you have to take every project that comes across your desk. Fortunately, that is not the case.

According to a recent report by the *Wall Street Journal*, those individuals who are self-employed are able to request between 20 and 40 percent more for their services than people who are doing the same type of job with a corporation. The reason is simple. The clients do not have to pay self-employed people for unemployment compensation, workers' compensation, or employee benefits, such as health insurance and sick leave.

As an employed individual, your federal and state taxes are withheld from your paycheck. When you are self-employed, you generally pay your taxes on a quarterly basis, which means you are able to hold on to your money longer before paying it to the Internal Revenue Service (IRS). The key is to make sure you have enough money to pay your estimated taxes.

Self-employed individuals also enjoy several tax deductions that employed people do not. Your business expenses – including new computers, print cartridges, paper, pens, travel expenses, insurance, and business-related meals and entertainment – are all tax deductible. Unfortunately, employed people are not eligible for such deductions.

Think of it this way. If you are an employee, you must put gas in your car so you can drive to and from work. That gas is *not* deductible. But, if you are self-employed, you can deduct expenses for all travel that is work-related, not just driving back and forth to an office. Remember, though, that you must keep good records and always keep your receipts.

As a self-employed individual, you will have to consider how you are going to save for retirement. Fortunately, the self-employed enjoy tax benefits on such open retirement plans as SEP-IRA and the Keogh Plan. These plans are designed to shelter substantial amounts of money for the self-employed so that they will have adequate money to live on when they retire.

With all the monetary benefits you will enjoy being self-employed, you will likely be pleasantly surprised to discover that you actually are paying less in taxes than when you were employed.

Of course, there are other benefits you will enjoy when you are self-employed. First, you can choose to work where you want: You can work from home, or you can rent an office. If you work from home, you will no longer have to worry about waking up extra early in the morning to fight rush-hour traffic.

Working from home or working in your own office means you also no longer have to worry about stressful and sometimes messy office politics. You also do not have to deal with office gossip.

Unless you come into contact with clients on a daily basis, you also will not have to spend money on a full wardrobe. You can wear what you want. If you want to work in your pajamas, you can. If you want to work in the middle of the night, you can. You have a lot more freedom when you are self-employed than you do when you are working for someone else.

The Bad – Disadvantages of Working for Yourself

Working for yourself has distinct advantages, but there are some disadvantages as well. Remember, however, there are disadvantages to every job and business situation. The question is, Do the benefits outweigh the disadvantages for *you*?

Pay is contingent upon you working. One distinct disadvantage of self-employment is payment. When you are an employee, you get paid regardless of whether business is slow or not. When you are self-employed, you only make money as long as you work. You must prepare, and save, for the slow times. Every business – and every self-employed person – goes through slow periods. If you are prepared for that eventuality, you will have a much easier time dealing with it when it arrives.

Benefits. You will have to pay for all your own benefits when you are self-employed, unless you have a spouse or a partner who can put you on his or her health insurance, for example. Benefits generally include health insurance and retirement plans. If you cannot afford health insurance or putting money into your retirement savings, you will have to go without those benefits. As you start to make more money, you then can focus on giving yourself benefits. If you are injured while self-employed, you will want to have unemployment and workers' compensation to fall back on.

Equipment. An employer is required to supply space and equipment so that employees can perform their jobs. As a self-employed individual, you also must have all your own equipment, such as a computer and whatever tools you need to provide the particular services you offer.

If you do not have the needed equipment, you must purchase it. The good news is that your equipment will likely be tax deductible.

Federal and state laws. There are federal and state laws that protect employees from unfair work practices, and employers are required to pay minimum wage and overtime to prohibit discrimination and harassment. They must also provide leave for family emergencies, military service, voting, and jury duty. There are very few federal laws like these that apply to the self-employed.

You must keep good records. As a self-employed individual, you will be required to file in-depth tax returns, which means two things. First, you must strictly adhere to a good recordkeeping system; if you are audited and have failed to record payments or other important information, you could find yourself in trouble.

Second, if you are not well versed in filling out your tax returns, you will need to have an accountant or other tax expert take care of it for you.

It is difficult to take out loans. Unfortunately, as a self-employed individual, you might find yourself discriminated against by lenders. Because you do not have a guaranteed income, at least in the beginning, you are going to find it very difficult to get banks, insurers, lenders, and other businesses to agree to do business with you. Or, if they do agree to give you a loan, they may charge much more than they would if you had a steady job.

As a result, you likely will have a difficult time taking out car loans, mortgages, and other types of loans, because you will have to show your annual income, often for a period of several years.

You may pay more for health insurance. Health insurance, unless you have a pre-existing condition, is often easy to get, but you are going to pay more for it than you would as an employee in a large company with group rates. Depending on your deductible, you (as half of a couple) could be charged several hundred dollars or more a month for health insurance.

CASE STUDY: DR. LARINA KASE

Larina Kase, Psy.D., M.B.A., is a licensed psychologist, a success coach, a *New York Times* bestselling author, and an experienced media source. Her primary areas of expertise include managing emotions, communicating at your best, influencing others through leadership, and using psychology to build your business.

Dr. Kase is a great example for people who want to break away from a nine-to-five job to start a business. She started her executive coaching company while she was employed with another company. Her business grew quickly, and she decided she wanted to be in control and go out on her own. It was a very difficult decision, she says, because she had to say goodbye to her "real job" forever, and she was nervous about not having colleagues or a support network. She knew that if she did not leave, she would not be able to achieve her goals. The turning point came, she says, when she no longer had the time to market her business and still maintain the other job. So she took the plunge, making the short-term sacrifice of a stable income for the benefit of seeing her goals become a reality.

In the beginning, Dr. Kase made lots of mistakes. One of her biggest mistakes, she says, was that she wanted to do things cheaply. She soon discovered that you sacrifice quality by going cheap. She found someone to do a Web site for $150. Later, she was asked to be on a national TV show and had to show her Web site to thousands of

---

CASE STUDY: DR. LARINA KASE

people. She lost the opportunity to present a great Web site on national television. Dr. Kase recommends that you approach your business as a business and not be afraid to invest money. Like a child or a pet, you have to feed your business to make it grow.

She also suggests that you begin your business by creating a business plan with both short-term and long-term goals. Most important, include a great marketing plan, as that will be your key to growth.

Larina Kase, Psy.D., M.B.A.
President
Performance & Success Coaching LLC
www.pascoaching.com
www.larinakase.com

Dr. Larina Kase (see case study above) is an expert in the field of business coaching and works with clients to help them conquer their fears. As you think about starting your own small business, you are probably anxious and afraid. Your fear, Dr. Kase says, may or may not be founded on fact. In many cases, you may be fearful because you do not have the information you need or because you do not know what to do to get started. You may have a good technical background in your subject but little knowledge of business. Here are some tips from Dr. Kase on conquering your fear:

1. Instead of worrying, find the information you need or pay someone to help you get the information to start your business.

2. Find supporters who can help you in times of doubt and fear.

3. Ask yourself, "Is it worth it for me to conquer this fear?" In other words, are the rewards worth the costs of working on the fear? In some cases, the answer may be no. If the answer is yes, however, and you must do it, then get started.

4. When you experience fear, be aware of how you are responding to it. In many cases, the fear may be causing you to make decisions that

limit your business growth. For example, you may be worried about your financial situation; as a result, you may limit expenditures just when you need to spend in order to grow.

5. Get objective, outside opinions from knowledgeable individuals as you consider your business. Listening to the advice of others will help confirm to you that you are on the right track.

Finally, Dr. Kase provides some advice for dealing with the objects of your fear. First, make a list of your fears, ordering them from "a little intimidating but manageable" to "completely terrifying." Then work through the list, starting with the smaller fears and building up to the things you fear the most. By the time you reach the bigger fears, you will have had lots of practice, and you will be less terrified. The fears that seemed overwhelming in the beginning will seem manageable in the end.

It Can Be a Little Worse Than Bad

Many people who are self-employed institute a policy requiring clients to pay a deposit, often 50 percent, before they begin work. One of the biggest risks an independent contractor takes is doing work for a client without first getting the full payment or a deposit up front.

If you complete work for a client who does not pay, you have several options for getting your money. You can file a lawsuit in small-claims court for the cost of the work you completed plus court costs, or you can report the amount you are owed as an unpaid account with the credit bureaus. Both could light a fire under and convince your client to pay you what you are owed.

Always have a signed and dated contract when working with any client, even a client you have worked with repeatedly in the past. A signed and dated contract protects you, especially if you need to take a client to court to get paid.

Unfortunately, when you are self-employed, you have to pay double the Social Security and Medicare taxes of your employed counterparts. Employees pay only 7.65 percent of their salary, up to a set limit that changes every year. Employers then match the amount their employees pay.

When you are self-employed, you have to pay the entire tax yourself; that is 15.3 percent of your income, in addition to your federal and state income taxes. Certain deductions can help bring this amount down. To learn more, visit the Social Security Administration at **www.socialsecurity.gov**.

As an employee, you may be laid off if the company or business fails, but you are not directly responsible for any unpaid bills it may have. If you are a self-employed sole proprietor, you are personally liable for any business debts you may incur. You can lose much of what you own if your business fails and you owe creditors or others. Fortunately, if you have insurance, your personal exposure to loss may be decreased.

Do You Have What It Takes to Make It in Self-Employment?

Many people think they know what to expect from self-employment and thus believe that it is the life for them. The reality of self-employment is often much less glamorous than what some people envision.

The truth is, as you will read repeatedly throughout this book, self-employment requires a lot of hard work and time. In some cases, it can take several months, or even years, for a self-employed individual's income to meet and exceed the amount of money he or she earned as an employee. Unless you already have a full client base or people who have committed to providing you with work, you will have to build and cultivate your client list. This takes time, determination, and commitment.

Before you decide to quit your day job for self-employment, you must determine why you want to be self-employed. Start by asking yourself the following questions:

- Are you opting for self-employment because you want to be your own boss?

- Are you bored with your traditional nine-to-five job?

- Are you seeking an opportunity to do what you want, when you want, and how you want?

- Do you believe that self-employment will help improve your standard of living?

- Do you want a challenge?

- Are you ready to take control of your life and your career?

Once you know why you want to be self-employed, you will be able to determine if you have what it takes to make the transformation from employee to independent contractor (freelancer, consultant, or entrepreneur – whatever term you prefer).

Realize, however, that you do not need all the traits of a successful entrepreneur and self-employed individual right away. You may not have all the skills you need right now, but you certainly can work on acquiring them. For example, your organizational skills may not be as strong as they could be. While you are improving your organizational skills, you can hire someone who is strong in that area to help you.

To determine if you have what it takes to work for yourself, start by thinking about and answering the following questions:

Do you have the time required? Self-employed people generally work far more hours than their employed counterparts, especially in the beginning. Are you willing to sacrifice your social life in the short-term to reach your long-term goal of becoming successful in self-employment? If you have a family, are you and they willing to sacrifice your time together so you can concentrate on building your client base and getting enough work to sustain you?

Do you have the patience? Becoming successful in self-employment, as we have mentioned previously, can take time – anywhere from several months to several years. Do you have the patience required to build your business?

Do you have the funds? Making the transition from employee to independent contractor is a huge leap. Do you have the funds to sustain you (and your family) while you are building your business? The general rule of thumb is that you should have sufficient funds to sustain you and your family for at least six months before you quit your nine-to-five job for self-employment. It may take that long for you to begin making enough money to cover all your expenses. Also, you may have an unexpected emergency that those funds will help cover.

Do you have a place to work? As we will discuss later in the book, you can work either from your home or from a rented office. If you do not want to shell out the money for rented space in the beginning, do you have space in your home to work?

If you have a spare bedroom, you may be able to convert it into an office, or you can transform part of another room into your working space. Keep in mind that, when determining where you will work, you want to pick a space that will allow you to work effectively. For example, you do not want your office space in the middle of a popular space, like your living room. You want office space that allows you the quiet you need to get your work done.

Are you a self-starter? Compared to the self-employed, employees have it relatively easy. Bosses are there to remind them of looming deadlines and of what projects have the highest priority. To succeed in self-employment, you must be a self-starter. You will not have a boss standing over your shoulder, demanding you get your work done. It is all up to you.

Self-employment requires discipline, motivation, and strong organizational skills.

Are you motivated? Even with the hard work and long hours often required in self-employment, working for yourself can be an exhilarating, rewarding experience. Yet it also can be a roller coaster ride with many ups and downs. You will find challenges and obstacles at every turn. Do you have the drive to keep going forward even when things are not going your way?

It is important to understand and acknowledge that you will go through periods of burnout. When you are clearly focused on your goal and motivated, you will better be able to make it through those difficult times.

Are you a leader? To be a successful independent contractor, you must be a strong leader. If you feel more comfortable being a follower, the self-employed life likely is not for you. You must have confidence in your ability to get the job done and achieve your goals.

You may come to a point where you have too much work and decide that you want to farm work out to another independent contractor, or you may even want to hire employees. In both situations, you must be a strong leader.

Are you competitive? You must find work for yourself, and most fields (e.g., writing, public relations, Web design, and so on) are highly competitive. Are you competitive in nature and willing to do the work required to win the clients and the work you need?

Can you make decisions? It might sound like a simple, even ridiculous question, but there are people who simply cannot make sound decisions. As a self-employed individual, you will have to make decisions constantly, and sometimes you will have to make them very quickly and/or under extremely stressful circumstances. Are you a decision maker?

Do you know how to organize and plan? When you are self-employed, you essentially are running your own business. For a business to thrive, its owner must be able to organize and plan for the short term and the long term. You have likely heard the old saying, "Fail to plan and plan to fail." It is true, especially when it comes to business. The Small Business Administration cites failure to plan and inadequate organization as major reasons for small business failures.

Are you client-oriented? As a self-employed individual, you are going to be dealing with clients on a daily basis. Ultimately, your success comes down to two things: your ability to attract new clients and the skill required to keep them happy with your work.

One of the best ways to gain new business is through word of mouth. If you have satisfied clients, they are going to be inclined to recommend your services to others.

Again, before you make the leap from employed to self-employed, make sure you think about the realities of self-employed life and what it takes to be successful as an independent contractor. When you are certain self-employment is a road you want to take, you will be ready to start preparing for the transition.

CASE STUDY: DR. LINDA JOHNSON, D.D.S.

After almost 30 years of practicing and owning two practices, Dr. Linda Johnson has found success as a dentist, but it has come at a price. She says her biggest mistakes have come from personnel issues. Mainly, she had been too slow to fire people and had left finances

---

CASE STUDY: DR. LINDA JOHNSON, D.D.S.

in the care of incompetent individuals. The qualities Dr. Johnson believes are most important for successful business owners are:

- Discipline: Do the hard work and put in the time to make your business successful. "You just can't get sick," she says.

- Study: Learn the trends in your industry and know your market.

- Be frugal: Understand that you have to spend money to make money.

Small-business owners, she says, must be able to deal with uncertainty, make decisions, and live with the consequences. You have all the responsibility for those decisions: "The buck stops with you!"

Dr. Johnson practices in Palm Harbor, Florida. She can be reached through her professional Web site, **www.lindajeanjohnson.com.**

Beware: Scams Aimed at the Self-Employed

Everyone wants to get rich quickly. Unfortunately, unless you are extremely lucky and in the right place at the right time, in all likelihood you are not going to get rich without a great deal of time, money, and effort. But there are plenty of people, especially online, who want you to believe that you can make a lot of money in very little time and with very little effort.

The Internet is awash with people looking for golden opportunities and with predators eager to take advantage of those people. Keep that in mind as you move into the world of self-employment.

If you run across an opportunity that sounds too good to be true, it probably is. If you are in doubt about an offer, here are some suggestions to help you evaluate it:

1. Check to see if the organization is a member of the Better Business Bureau (BBB). If it is, it has been evaluated by the BBB, and you can check its customer service record.

2. The National Consumers League (**www.nclnet.org**) has a fraud section that monitors Internet fraud and provides fraud tips, at **www .fraud.org/internet/inttip/inttip.htm**. You may find information about the company you are looking at on this site.

3. Ask the company for referrals from satisfied customers. Then check out the referrals to be sure they are legitimate. Talk to the customers to be sure they are real and ask them about the services provided by the company.

4. Stop and think: Is what the company is selling so valuable it cannot be found elsewhere? Can I do this myself? The answer to the first question is often no, and to the second question it is yes.

How You Can Use This Book

The Complete Guide to Working for Yourself is designed to help you with issues from starting your business to dealing with the ongoing legal and tax issues that every self-employed individual faces. What is more, this book's goal is to make your experience in self-employment the best it possibly can be.

If you have never worked for yourself, or if you are just starting out, you will learn everything you need to know to begin the process of making the transformation from employee to self-employed individual.

If you already have a business, you can most certainly benefit from the information in *The Complete Guide to Working for Yourself*, including ensuring what you are doing is correct. *The Complete Guide to Working for Yourself* is an excellent resource if you have questions or need to verify you are doing something properly.

chapter 2

Choosing Your Legal Entity

One of the most important decisions you will have to make is what type of legal business entity, or business structure, you want to create your business under.

Because the legal entity you choose will have a powerful impact on your business in the long term, the Small Business Administration recommends consulting an attorney or an accountant to determine which ownership structure best meets your needs.

The legal entity you choose affects how you are taxed, whether or not you will be responsible for your business debts, and how your business will be treated by the IRS. Until you decide on a legal entity and file the proper paperwork in the state where you will be doing business, you cannot legally operate your business. So it is important to decide on a legal entity before you begin operations.

Deciding on a Legal Form of Business

There are several questions you should ask yourself during the decision-making process, including:

- How big do you want your business to grow?

- How much control do you want over your business?

- What are the tax implications of each ownership structure?

- Will you have to invest your business earnings back into the business?

- How much vulnerability are you willing to expose your business to?

- How much personal liability are you willing to assume for the debts of the business?

- What are your expected profits for your business?

- What are your expected losses for your business?

There are four basic types of business structures, with variations of several of these types. The basic types are:

- Sole proprietorship

- Corporation (S-corporation or C-corporation)

- Partnership

- Limited liability company (LLC)

If you are the sole owner of the business, you will not choose a partnership as your legal entity, because partnerships must have a minimum of two owners. Therefore, as sole owner, you will have to decide whether sole proprietorship, a limited liability company, or a corporation will suit your needs.

Your choice ultimately will determine how you will organize your business. The good news is you can change your legal business structure down the line. You, like many other self-employed people, may very well start as a sole proprietor. As your business grows and becomes established, you then may decide to make the switch to a limited liability company or a corporation. It is usually easy to move from a simpler form of legal entity, like a sole proprietorship, to a more complex form, like a corporation. It is not as easy to dissolve a corporation and become a sole proprietorship.

Sole Proprietorships

A sole proprietorship is a one-owner business. It is the easiest business entity to create, and it is the easiest to dissolve. As a sole proprietor, you do not have to get permission from the government to form your business, and you are not required to pay any fees to establish the sole proprietorship. Once you fill out the required paperwork, you start doing business.

The vast majority of self-employed individuals function as sole proprietors, and most of them run small operations. According to the U.S. Department of the Treasury, there were almost 20 million sole proprietorships in the United States, with combined receipts of over $950 million, in 2000. A sole proprietor is able to hire employees or use independent contractors or freelancers. Some health care professionals (e.g., chiropractors, optometrists, podiatrists) with employees and large offices set up their practices as sole proprietorships. Just because you are a sole proprietor does not mean your business has to be small.

Tax Concerns

As a sole proprietor, you are your business for tax purposes. You do not have to pay taxes or file your taxes separately from your business; you simply file one tax return. You report your income and your losses from the business on your personal tax return. If you are earning money as a self-employed person, you will add your business income to any other income you may have. For example, if you file a joint tax return with a spouse, you add your business income to your spouse's income, and you are taxed on the total.

If you have incurred a business loss, you can use that loss to offset income from other sources.

The IRS will want to know the profitability of your business, so you will need to file an IRS Schedule C *Profit or Loss From Business* form as part of your personal tax return. If you have multiple businesses, you have to file either a Schedule C or another appropriate tax return form for each business.

As a business owner, you do not pay payroll taxes on your income, nor do you withhold income tax. You do have to pay self-employment taxes (Social Security and Medicare taxes) on your net profit from your business. These taxes, along with your income taxes, must be paid four times a year as estimated taxes. If you do professional work for clients, they do not withhold taxes from the amount they pay you, but they must file a Form 1099-MISC to report the payment to the IRS if the total annual payment to you is over $600.

Example: Troy runs his freelance writing business as a sole proprietor. He must report the income that he receives from his clients on his individual tax return (IRS Form 1040) and file a Schedule C showing his business income and expenses and his net income or loss from the business. He does not have to file a separate tax return for his business. Last year, he earned $50,000 from writing but had $10,000 in expenses. As a result, he had a net income of $40,000. He reported the gross income from writing ($50,000) and his business expenses ($10,000) on a Schedule C. He added the $40,000 profit to his income from other sources and reported the total income on his Form 1040. He must pay income tax and self-employment taxes based on his net income amount ($40,000).

If Troy's freelancing business had a $10,000 loss, he would not have to pay income tax or self-employment tax on that loss, but his other sources of income would still be taxable.

Liability Concerns

Another concern that you will have as a business owner is liability. Liability is the extent of legal responsibility you have for paying your business's debts, including judgments entered against the business in lawsuits.

As a sole proprietor, you are personally responsible for all business debts you incur. If you owe a business creditor, the creditor can go after your personal and business assets to collect the debt. If your business owes money, your creditor(s) can take your personal money from your bank account, or you can lose your house or your car. The creditor can take whatever is needed to ensure your debts are repaid. The same is true for personal creditors. They can go after both personal and business assets, including business accounts and equipment.

There are several types of business-related lawsuits that may affect you, including:

- **Premises liability:** You are responsible for injuries or damages that occur at your office, workshop, or other place of business.

- **Infringement liability:** Someone claims that you have infringed on a copyright, trademark, patent, or trade secret.

- **Employer liability:** You are liable for injuries or damages caused by employees while they are working for you.

- **Product liability:** You are responsible for injuries or damages caused by the product you manufactured or sold to the public.

- **Negligence liability:** Someone claims that you failed to use "reasonable care" in your actions, which resulted in injuries or damages.

It is important that you understand the different lawsuits that may affect you. You should not worry too much about lawsuits if you purchase business property, casualty, and liability insurance. The risk of having to pay off business debts cannot be insured and probably will have to be paid from your personal assets if the business cannot pay its debts.

Audits

As a self-employed person, you will be considered an independent contractor by most of your clients. If your relationship with a client appears to be an employer-employee relationship, the government may call you an employee of the client. An employee status may cause tax consequences for both parties, including heavy fines or back taxes. For this reason, most clients will only hire self-employed people who are independent contractors and are viewed as such by the government.

Advantages and Disadvantages to Sole Proprietorships

As with all business entities, there are distinct advantages and disadvantages to sole proprietorships.

The advantages of a sole proprietorship include:

- Starting a sole proprietorship is easy; it is the easiest business structure to form.

- Creating a sole proprietorship is inexpensive.

- Sole proprietors only file one individual tax return.

- As a sole proprietor, you make all the decisions for your business.

- It is generally quite easy to dissolve a sole proprietorship.

Of course, you also should be aware of the disadvantages of a sole proprietorship, such as the following:

- Sole proprietors may not be able to obtain loans and often must use personal savings or consumer loans to fund their businesses.

- Sole proprietors have a difficult time securing funds from investors, who prefer the protections of corporate and LLC business forms.

- Being responsible for all business decisions is listed as an advantage to sole proprietorship; however, it also can be a disadvantage, depending on your personality.

- If something happens to you, the business may cease to exist.

Setting Up a Sole Proprietorship

Setting up a sole proprietorship is easy and inexpensive. If you have no employees and are operating under your own name, you will only need to have a business checking account. You may want to check with the city and county where your business is located to see if they require a license for your specific type of business.

If you have employees, you will need an Employer ID Number (EIN), which can be obtained from the IRS by filling out an SS-4 form. If you are not operating under your own name, you will need to go to the county where your business is located and complete a "DBA" or "fictitious name" statement. For example, if your name is Susan Cosgrove and your business name is Best Carpet Cleaning, you will need a DBA statement so people in your community know who is operating Best Carpet Cleaning. If you are not sure if you need to file a DBA, check with the county recorder's office.

Partnerships

If you work with another individual and you are not the sole owner of your business, you should set up a partnership, unless you form a corporation or limited liability corporation. A partnership is similar to a sole proprietorship, except that there are two or more owners. Like a sole proprietorship, a partnership is legally inseparable from the owners. Partnerships do not pay taxes as an entity, but they do file an annual information tax form, called a 1065. Partnership income and losses are passed through the partnership to the partners and reported on their individual tax returns according to the percentage of ownership for each partner. For example, if there are two partners, one with 70 percent ownership and the other with 30 percent ownership, the total net income is split between the partners 70/30. Partners are required to file IRS Schedule E forms, which show their partnership income and deductions, with their returns.

The main difference between partnerships and sole proprietors is that both partners have to make tough decisions as to the following:

- How each partner shares in the profits or losses

- How partnership decisions are made

- How disputes will be resolved

- Each partner's duties

- What happens if a partner leaves the business, dies, or becomes unable to continue as a partner

You should create a written partnership agreement covering each of these issues. While it is not legally required, it is important to cover all possible circumstances before they occur. Having an attorney prepare a partnership agreement may save both the friendship and the partnership.

Liability

Each partner is personally liable for all partnership debts and lawsuits. You are personally liable for any business debt that your partner incurs, whether or not you know about those debts.

A limited partnership allows one or more general partners to run the business, but the limited partner only invests in the business and does not help run the business. The limited partners are similar to shareholders in a corporation. They are not personally liable for the partnership's debts. The general partners are just like normal partners and are liable. General partnerships are popular in real estate and similar investments.

Professionals may also set up registered limited liability partnerships (RLLPs) in some states. Certain states do not allow professionals to set up limited liability companies, and RLLPs are an alternative. They give partners the same type of limited liability as owners of a professional corporation. They are personally liable for their own malpractice but not that of the other partners as long as the other partners are acting independently. The RLLP also receives protection from business debts, lawsuits, and other suits. These partnerships often are limited to health care professionals, legal professionals, and accountants.

Advantages and Disadvantages of Partnerships

Before forming a partnership, consider both the advantages and the disadvantages of the legal business structure. The following are several advantages to a partnership:

- Partnerships are relatively easy to form. You will, however, have to spend considerable time and money to have an attorney craft a partnership agreement.

- You should have an easier time raising funds for the business because there are at least two people running the business.

- Each partner files individual tax returns.

- Partnerships have relatively low startup costs.

Several disadvantages to partnerships include the following:

- You are legally responsible for each of your partner's actions.

- Partners must share profits.

- All decisions must be agreed to by all partners, making internal conflict a real possibility.

- If a partner quits the business, dies, or becomes unable to continue as a partner, the partnership can legally be dissolved.

- It may be difficult to find investors for a partnership.

Limited Liability Companies

The limited liability company, introduced in the 1990s, is the newest business structure in the United States. Owners of LLCs are called "members." LLCs are taxed like a sole proprietorship or a partnership, but they have the advantage of a corporation in protecting the members from liability. Because LLCs are easy to form and run, they quickly have become popular with the self-employed.

In the past, most states required LLCs to have two or more owners. However, all states now permit one-person limited liability companies, where you are considered a business owner and not an employee. If you receive a guaranteed salary or pay from the LLC, you are considered an employee of the LLC. If you guarantee yourself $10,000 per year, regardless of the company's profits, you are treated as an employee, and that annual income is subject to income tax withholding and self-employment taxes.

There are several states that require certain professionals – those in the health care industry, attorneys, engineers, and accountants – to form a "professional LLC." Those who run a professional LLC must follow special rules, and each member is required to carry a designated amount of malpractice insurance. There are also those states that require professionals to form a limited liability partnership (LLP) rather than an LLC. Check with your Secretary of State to determine your state's particular rules and requirements.

Because many states do not protect LLC owners from personal liability for the malpractice of another professional in the company, LLC owners can be held personally liable for the malpractice of one of their coworkers. For this reason, professionals generally find it is not advantageous to form LLCs.

Taxes

If the LLC has only one member, the LLC is treated as a sole proprietorship for tax purposes. The member reports profits, losses, and deductions on his Schedule C. If the LLC has more than one member, the business is required to prepare and file IRS Form 1065 *Partnership Return of Income*, which shows the allocation of profits, losses, credits, and deductions that have been passed through to the members. The LLC is required to prepare and distribute a Schedule K-1 to show the membership's allocations.

IRS rules allow LLC owners to decide how they want the LLC taxed. LLCs can be, and often are, taxed as a pass-through entity (that is, with its income passing through to the members). As a pass-through entity, an LLC files an informational tax return, and the profits and losses are reported on the tax returns of the LLC member or members.

Limited liability companies can also be taxed as C or S corporations. When an LLC is taxed as a C or S corporation, the members make an "election" to receive corporation tax treatment with the IRS. You can save on employment taxes if you choose this option, and you can maximize deductions for fringe benefits. Still, very few businesses make this election.

To make an election, you must check the appropriate box on IRS Form 8832, *Entity Classification Election*. This election can be made at any time. Your business is treated exactly like a C corporation once you make the election. You will be required to file corporate tax returns, and you will have all the benefits and disadvantages of the C corporation tax treatment.

If you want your business treated as an S corporation, you will file IRS Form 2553, *Election by a Small Business Corporation*. You must meet all the conditions of an S corporation before you are allowed to make this election. Your business is still an LLC for non-tax purposes. You can also choose to switch or make another election, but you are required to wait five years before you are allowed to do so.

Advantages and Disadvantages of Limited Liability Companies

As with every business structure, LLCs have their advantages and their disadvantages. Carefully consider both the pros and the cons of the LLC before deciding whether it is the best legal structure for your business.

Advantages of the LLC include:

- LLC members enjoy the same limited liability from business debts and lawsuits as corporations. LLCs are often favored over partnerships because they offer the same tax benefits while also providing limited liability to the individual members.

- An LLC takes less time and costs less than creating a corporation.

- An LLC is generally easier to run than a corporation. Corporations must hold meetings and adhere to other formalities, while LLCs are more flexible in their day-to-day management.

- An LLC has more flexibility in allocating profits and losses among the business's owners. S corporations have to pay taxes on profits or receive the benefits of losses in proportion to their stock ownership. For example, if the S corporation has two shareholders and each owns 50 percent of the stock, they must pay tax on 50 percent of the corporation's profits or get the benefits of 50 percent of the losses. An LLC offers the flexibility of adjusting this however the members decide.

- Unlike an LLC, a C corporation is unable to allocate profits and losses to shareholders. In a corporation, shareholders receive a financial return through dividends or a share in assets when the business is sold or liquidated.

- LLCs do not have any special rules, as the S corporation has, when it comes to who can and who cannot form the business.

- LLC members are not employees and thus do not have to pay federal or state unemployment taxes. However, you must pay these taxes if you are the only employee of a corporation.

Among the disadvantages of the LLC are:

- LLC members are required to pay self-employment taxes on the income they receive, even if the income is in the form of a distribution. You can save on self-employment taxes if you form an S corporation, because distributions are not subject to self-employment taxes.

- Firms that hire LLCs and pay them more than $600 per year must file Form 1099-MISC with the IRS to report the payment. However, this rule does not apply if the LLC is taxed as a corporation.

- If a member of an LLC goes into bankruptcy, dies, or becomes unable to participate, the LLC is automatically dissolved, unless the members have taken care to include provisions for continuation in the operating agreement.

- While setting up an LLC is generally straightforward and simple, you will have to fill out paperwork that is more complex than that of a sole proprietorship or a partnership.

Forming an LLC

To form an LLC you must file articles of organization with your appropriate state agency, usually the Secretary of State. Your business name must also have the words "limited liability company," "LLC," "LC," or a similar phrase, depending on your state law.

Although it is not required by the state, an LLC should also have an operating agreement, similar to a partnership agreement. This document describes the way the LLC operates, the responsibilities of members, ownership percentages, and what happens in certain circumstances. An attorney should prepare this agreement under your direction.

Corporations

The word *corporation* often conjures thoughts of large corporations like Wal-Mart or Microsoft. However, your business does not have to be worth or make billions of dollars to be incorporated. Any business can become a corporation, even if that business only has one owner. Generally, most corporations have several owners; such corporations often are referred to as "closely held corporations."

While it is not a popular business structure for self-employed individuals, you may want to consider the benefits a corporation will offer you. For example, incorporating often will save you money on taxes and limit your liability.

A corporation is a legal form of business that allows the business owners to share in the profits and losses. As a corporation, your business has a distinct and separate existence from you, the owner. It may hold title to property; it may sue others (it can also be sued); and it can have bank accounts. In addition, the business can borrow money, hire employees, and operate as a person would in the business world. In theory, a corporation will exist in three groups, although the same person can operate in all three functions. These groups include:

- **Directors direct the overall business.** Directors are members of the board of directors, serving as advisors and policy makers for the business.

- **Officers run the day-to-day affairs.** The officers usually include a chief executive officer, a president, and other lesser officers.

- **Shareholders have invested in the business by purchasing stock.** Usually small businesses issue only a small amount of stock and are privately held, as opposed to big corporations that issue large amounts of stock to the public.

Again, a sole person can fulfill all these roles and hold all the corporate stock. You do not have to recruit a board of directors or hire officers to run your business. You can do it all yourself if your business is small. But before you decide not to have a board of directors, think about the important role these people might be able to play in your business, such as advising you and providing you with a sounding board for decisions. Often, an attorney, a certified public accountant (CPA) or financial advisor, and mentors are asked to serve on the board.

When your business is incorporated, you will be considered an employee of the business. You also may be an officer or shareholder and be on the board of directors. As an employee, even if you are an officer (president, for example), you will be paid a salary. As a member of the board of directors, you participate in the decisions of the business. As a shareholder, you can vote your shares of stock. Most business owners hold the majority of shares for themselves so they can control the business.

When a client hires you, the client actually is hiring your incorporated business. You often will have to sign a written agreement with the client on behalf of the corporation. When the client pays you, the check is made payable to the corporation and is deposited into the corporation's bank account rather than your personal bank account. You then pay yourself from the corporate funds as salary, bonus, and dividends.

You are required to withhold Social Security and Medicare from your salary as an employee. You then must pay the taxes to the IRS as your employer would if you were an employee at another business. The total of Social Security and Medicare, unfortunately, is about the same you would pay as if you were a sole proprietor. The amount is just paid from two different accounts: the business account and the personal account. For example, if you are paid a salary of $100,000 a year, you would personally pay $7,650 in Social Security and Medicare taxes, through payroll withholding, and your company would pay $7,650 on your behalf as an employee. The full amount of Social Security and Medicare taxes are paid to the Social Security Administration and are credited to your Social Security account.

Because the money is yours, there is really no major difference between incorporation and sole proprietorship in this situation. One advantage, although it will cost you money, is that your corporation will be paying state unemployment taxes. This means that, if your corporation were to fail, you could draw unemployment.

Technically speaking, if you incorporate your business, you are not self-employed because you are an employee of the corporation. The corporation is not an employee of clients.

Audits

The self-employed are often at risk of being audited by the IRS, mainly due to claims that their clients have treated them as employees. As a corporation, there is a much smaller chance that you will be classified in this manner and, in turn, there is much less of a chance that you will be audited, often because it takes time and there is a complicated process involved in becoming incorporated.

In 1996, the status of those in the corporation as employees was confirmed by the IRS in the manual they issue to train auditors on how to determine the status of workers. The manual shows that the incorporated worker is not to be treated as an employee of the client, but as an employee of his corporation.

With this clear notation available, many hiring firms have sought out corporations over sole proprietors. These hiring firms often give preference to corporations when they are forced to make a decision between the two. They also are able to justify the time and the cost because the business is a corporation.

If you are a computer programmer, a systems analyst consultant, an engineer, or a drafter who performs technical services and you may be required to work on-site with your client, consider becoming incorporated to avoid any problems with being viewed as an employee. That way, the hiring firm is able to hire your corporation instead of hiring you personally.

However, do not get too comfortable just because your business is a corporation. An employee of the corporation also can be reclassified as an employee of a client or customer under IRS rules, if he or she does not follow corporate formalities or abuses the corporate form. The IRS may disregard your corporation status and claim you are acting as an employee if you:

- Deposit your earnings directly in your personal checking account instead of the corporate account

- Fail to file tax returns for the corporation

- Do not issue yourself stock

- Fail to follow corporate formalities, such as annual meetings, and do not keep corporate accounting records

For these and other reasons, it is important that you conduct your corporate business according to appropriate protocols, including:

- Setting up a board of directors and having regular meetings with minutes.

- Issuing stock to shareholders, even if there are only a few of these shareholders.

- Keeping your personal business and corporate business separate. As noted above, you need to be sure that all income goes through the corporation and that you are paid only as an employee.

Liability Concerns

A corporation provides the owners and shareholders with "limited liability" in theory. That is, the shareholders are not personally responsible for any business debt that the corporation incurs, nor are they personally responsible for any lawsuits dealing with the corporation. The main reason many people incorporate is so they can obtain this limited liability. Still, the protection that limited liability brings may not be as great as many people believe.

Limited liability is broken down into two sections: business debts and lawsuits.

Business debts: Corporations were created to protect the personal assets of people who invest in the business if the business fails or is unable to pay back its creditors. The corporation's owners (the shareholders) are also not personally liable for debts or lawsuits, in theory. However, they can lose their investments in the corporation. The creditors are not able to go after personal assets of owners or employees, such as bank accounts, homes, cars, and so forth.

This theory almost always will hold true in the case of very large corporations. For example, if you were to buy stock in Dell, you would not have to worry about Dell's creditors suing you to repay the corporation's debts. This does not always work for small corporations. In fact, large creditors, such as banks, will not allow you to shield your personal assets by incorporating. They often will demand that you guarantee your business loans and credit personally, which requires you to sign a legal document that pledges your personal assets to pay for your business debt if your business is to run short on cash or assets.

Example: Charlotte forms a corporation for her house-painting business. She goes to her bank and applies for a business credit card. After reading the application carefully, she finds a clause that states she will be personally liable for the credit card balance – even though the card is not going to be in her name. Charlotte asks that the bank remove this clause, but her request is denied because it is the bank's policy to require guarantees on small corporations such as Charlotte's. Charlotte chooses to sign the form, with the understanding that the bank will be able to sue her if she does not pay off the credit card. The bank is also able to take her personal assets, including money from her personal bank account.

Other creditors may require similar clauses in small businesses. If you lease an office or equipment, the creditor may require that you personally guarantee those items. The standard forms you may sign often will include a similar clause requiring the personal guarantee. For this reason, it is extremely important that you thoroughly read any agreements that you enter into. In some cases, you may be able to avoid this personal guarantee, but if your business does not pay its bills, it is not likely that other businesses will be willing to extend you credit.

Lawsuits: Forming a corporation is also supposed to shield you from personal liability in any business-related lawsuits. If you are a small-business owner, however, do not expect too much protection.

Business owners, even if the business is incorporated, are personally liable if they are negligent in a situation. The individuals that own the corporation, or the shareholders, are personally liable for damages caused by negligence. If you fill all three roles in the corporation, you are the only shareholder, so you are personally liable in negligent situations. Lawyers will take advantage of this fact if it will work in favor of their clients. If you form a corporation and you do not have the funds or insurance to pay for a legal claim, the lawyer will go after your personal assets and collect on them. There are several situations that may cause you to be sued personally, even if you are a corporation, including the following:

- The UPS driver slips and falls on your doorstep and breaks a leg. In this instance, you are sued because you failed to keep your premises safe.

- Your employee accidentally injures a person while running your errands. The injured person may sue you for negligently hiring, training, or supervising your employee.

- The product you manufactured, invented, or designed injures several people. Each person could sue you for negligence.

- Someone sues you claiming copyright violation; you can be held personally liable.

In these instances, it will not matter whether you are a corporation or not.

Another means through which you can be held personally liable is a legal decision called "piercing the corporate veil." In this situation, the court disregards the corporation itself and holds the owners legally liable for damage done by the corporation or for business debts. If you treat your corporation as your alter ego, rather than the separate legal entity that it is, you may be personally at risk.

Example: A corporation fails to contribute money to the corporation or does not issue stock. Instead, the money is used personally by the corporation's owners who commingle the money with their personal funds. They also do not hold their annual meetings and do not observe corporate formalities, such as keeping minutes.

As stated above, setting out and following strict protocols for corporate actions can help you avoid the appearance that you and the corporation are one and the same and may possibly save you from being named in a lawsuit against the corporation.

Insurance: Insurance is a very simple way to relieve yourself of this personal liability. An insurer will defend you in lawsuits and pay any settlements or damage awards up to a certain amount. The amount of coverage is determined by the policy you choose. All business owners should have their businesses insured, be they a sole proprietor, limited liability corporation, partnership, or corporation. In addition to insuring your business for liabilities, your business insurance policy should include coverage for property damage, damage to contents and equipment, and business interruption insurance, in case you cannot operate for a period of time. Liability insurance can protect you in many different situations. Although business insurance may protect you in these situations, insurance cannot protect you if you fail to pay your business debts.

Taxes

There are two different types of corporations, and this affects which federal income tax rules will apply:

- C corporations (regular corporations)

- S corporations (small-business corporations)

A C corporation pays taxes as a corporate entity. The S corporation's shareholders split the S corporation's tax burden. When you incorporate your business, you can choose either option. S corporations are best for small businesses that have a relatively small income or suffer losses. C corporations are best for successful businesses that see substantial profits.

When you form your corporation, it will be a C corporation by default. If you wish to elect to be an S corporation, you must file this election within a certain time; check with your tax accountant to be sure you do not miss the deadline for filing this election.

You will save money on taxes by incorporating, and you also may gain several other benefits, such as being audited less often. Even when a small corporation is audited, the IRS will not look as rigorously at the small corporation's tax deductions as it does for sole proprietors. If you are not sure which type of corporation is best for you, consult your accountant or tax professional.

Taxes for C Corporations

A C corporation is treated as a separate entity from the business owner for tax purposes. The C corporation must pay income taxes on the net income of the corporation and also must file its own tax returns on an IRS Form 1120 or Form 1120-A. The income tax rates are lower than individual rates at some income levels, which is often a benefit for business owners. C corporations may take the same deductions as a sole proprietorship to determine net profits, and they also receive some additional deductions.

When you form a C corporation, you are distinguishing two separate taxpayers: you and your corporation. You do not have to pay personal income tax on the income of your incorporated business until it pays you in the form of a salary, bonus, or dividend. It will allow you to split the income that your business earns with your corporation, which also allows you to save on income tax because the corporate tax rate may be lower than your personal tax rate. A C corporation will pay less income than an individual will on the first $75,000 of taxable income.

You also are allowed to keep up to $250,000 of your business earnings in the corporate account without a penalty. This rule allows you to use this money to expand, buy equipment, and pay your benefits. If you keep more than $250,000, you will have to pay an extra 15 percent tax that is called "accumulated earnings tax." The accumulated earnings tax is intended to discourage the corporation from sheltering too much of its earnings. Another substantial tax benefit is that you do not have to pay Social Security and Medicare taxes on your corporation's profits, which is a 15.3 percent tax on salaries that are paid to yourself and your employees, up to $97,500 as of 2007. If you keep $10,000 in your corporation rather than paying it to yourself as a salary, you can save $1,530 in taxes.

If you are a self-employed person engaged in a professional service, the IRS will define you as a "personal service corporation"(PSC) or "professional corporation" (PC). A PSC or PC is set up as a C corporation and is required to pay a flat 35 percent tax rate.

You are a PSC if you provide consultation services and give a client your advice or counsel, and all your stock is owned by consultants who are employees of the corporation. You are not a consultant if your client simply purchases something from you or someone else who works for you. Unfortunately, many self-employed people fall into this category and are taxed at this high, flat rate.

A C corporation also will qualify as a PSC if the stock is owned by corporate employees who hold one of these positions:

- Accounting

- Engineering

- Law

- Health services (e.g., doctors, chiropractors, and dentists)

- Actuarial science

- Performing arts

Income splitting is not an attractive option with this high, flat rate. These corporations are not subject to the 15.3 percent Social Security and Medicare tax, so there are modest tax benefits available. For example, if you are a PSC owner in the 25 percent tax bracket and you are paid $10,000 in salary, you have to pay 25 percent income tax on the $10,000, plus the 15.3 percent Social Security and Medicare tax, which comes out to

40.3 percent in taxes. If you were to leave the $10,000 in the PSC, the corporation would only pay the flat rate of 35 percent.

Social Security taxes are subject to an annual income ceiling, so the advantage of not having to pay these taxes disappears at higher income levels. For example, if you are a PSC owner and pay yourself a $125,000 annual salary, you will be in the 28 percent tax bracket. Therefore, you will have to pay a 2.9 percent Medicare tax on the entire amount and an additional 12.9 percent Social Security tax on the first $97,500. The earnings over $97,500 are not susceptible to the 12.9 percent Social Security tax. If the PSC pays another $10,000 in salary, that amount would be subject to 31.9 percent (28 percent plus 2.9 percent). If the money were left in the PSC, the corporation would pay 35 percent income tax.

COMPARISON OF TAX RATES FOR 2006 INDIVIDUAL AND CORPORATE RATES				
Taxable Income	Individual Rate (Single)	Individual Rate (Married Filing Jointly)	Corporate Rate (Not PSC)	Personal Service Corporation Rate
Up to $7,000	10%	10%	15%	35%
$7,551 to $15,100	15%	10%	15%	35%
$15,101 to $30,650	15%	15%	15%	35%
$30,651 to $50,000	25%	15%	15%	35%
$50,001 to $61,300	25%	15%	15%	35%
$61,301 to $74,200	25%	25%	25%	35%
$74,201 to $75,000	28%	25%	25%	35%
$75,001 to $100,000	28%	25%	34%	35%
$100,001 to $123,700	28%	25%	25%	35%
$123,701 to $154,800	28%	28%	39%	35%
$154,801 to $188,450	33%	28%	39%	35%
$188,451 to $335,000	33%	33%	39%	35%
$335,001 to $336,550	33%	33%	34%	35%
$336,551 to $10,000,000	35%	35%	34%	35%

These income tax brackets are adjusted annually to compensate for inflation. The IRS Publication 505, Tax Withholding and Estimated Tax, is available on the IRS Web site at **www.irs.gov.**

There are several additional benefits that your corporation can provide to its employees. These benefits then can be deducted from the corporation's income as a business expense. Other forms of business are not allowed to do this. Benefits include:

- Health insurance for you and your family

- Disability insurance

- Reimbursement on medical expenses not covered by insurance

- Deferred compensation plans

- Group term life insurance

- Retirement plans

- Death benefit payment up to $5,000

With insurance costs continually on the rise, deducting your health insurance is one of the best reasons for forming a C corporation. You are not required to include the value of premiums or other payments your corporation makes for your benefits in your personal income for income tax purposes.

Owners of S corporations are allowed to deduct all their health insurance premiums from their personal income tax, including what they pay for their spouses and dependents. This is a special personal deduction and is not considered a business deduction. However, the deduction does not reduce their income for Social Security and Medicare taxes.

An S corporation is not able to provide other fringe benefits. If the entity provides another fringe benefit, such as disability insurance, the owner is required to include its value and pay income taxes on it. The only way around this is if the owner hires the spouse as an employee and provides the spouse with benefits.

C corporations are able to take advantage of medical reimbursement plans and of medical expenses that are not covered by insurance. A C corporation is allowed to deduct these costs as a business expense. If a sole proprietor or the owner of an S corporation were to pay for uninsured health expenses out of his or her own account, the personal income tax deduction would be limited to only those amounts that exceed 7.5 percent of his or her adjusted gross income.

Another benefit of forming a C corporation is that the shareholders can borrow up to $10,000 for the corporation with no interest. If you borrow more than this, you have to pay interest or tax on the amount of interest you would have paid.

IRS tables determine the interest rates for these loans, and no other forms of business are allowed this benefit. Borrowing money from your own business is very attractive because the interest-free loan is not a taxable income for you. Sign a promissory note obligating you to pay the amount back to the corporation on a specific date for legality purposes and to verify the loan. The loan also should be a secured loan that is guaranteed by personal property, such as a house or car.

S Corporation Taxes

An S corporation is taxed like a sole proprietorship. It is not a separate taxpaying entity, and the corporate income and losses are passed directly to the shareholders, which may include you and other individuals. The shareholders are required to split taxable profits according to the shares of stock ownership and report this income on their personal tax returns.

An S corporation will not normally pay taxes but must file an information return on IRS Form 1120-S, which indicates how much the business earned and each shareholder's portion of income or losses.

S corporations are increasing in popularity. They can give you the best of both worlds, because you are taxed as a sole proprietor, but you have the limited liability of a corporation owner. Your taxes are also much easier to file, and you can save on Social Security and Medicare taxes.

You must report income or loss from your S corporation on your individual tax return, which means you can deduct business losses from income from other sources, including your spouse's income if you are married and filing a joint return. Doing so is not allowed with a C corporation, because the C corporation is a separate taxpaying entity. This can be helpful if you are a new business and just starting out and incurring losses. You can use these losses to reduce your taxable income.

Example: Kelly and Terry are a married couple who file a joint income tax return. Kelly earns $80,000 from her job, and Terry quit his job to start a new, self-employed business. He forms an S corporation with himself as the only shareholder and employee. In his first year, he makes $20,000 in net income from his business, but the business has $40,000 in expenses. Kelly and Terry report their loss of $20,000 on their joint tax return and subtract it from their total taxable income. Kelly's $80,000 income puts them in the 25 percent tax bracket, so they save $5,000 in income taxes.

When you are an S corporation, you are unable to split your income between two separate taxpaying entities. If the business does well, splitting the income can reduce your federal taxes, because C corporations often are able to pay less tax than individuals at certain income levels. The inability to do this with an S corporation is the only real drawback to this business entity. Most new businesses do not make enough money to even consider income splitting, and if your business becomes particularly profitable, you can convert your business from an S corporation to a C corporation later on.

One important tax benefit is that an S corporation is able to save you Social Security and Medicare taxes. These taxes are a flat 15.3 percent on the first $97,500 of income that you have. If you make more than this in a year, you do not have to continue paying Social Security, but you must continue to pay 2.9 percent for Medicare. All businesses are required to pay these taxes, except the C corporation, which pays half and then you pay half. With an S corporation you report your corporation's earnings on your personal tax return. You must pay Social Security and Medicare on any employee salary that the S corporation pays you. You do not have to pay this tax on distributions from your S corporation. This means that the more net profits you pass through the corporation to yourself, the less Social Security and Medicare taxes you are required to pay.

Example: Mike, a consultant, forms an S corporation. He is the only shareholder and employee. In one year he has a net income of $40,000. If Mike pays this entire amount himself, he and his corporation will be required to pay 15.3 percent in taxes, or $6,120. If Mike pays himself a $20,000 salary, the remaining $20,000 is passed through the S corporation and is reported as an S corporation distribution on Mike's income tax return. Because this is a distribution and not employee earnings, Mike does not have to pay Social Security and Medicare taxes on this amount. Instead he pays $3,060 and saves $3,060.

In theory, if you were allowed to not pay yourself a salary, you would not have to pay any Social Security or Medicare. Of course, the IRS does not allow this. The IRS requires the S corporation shareholder-employees to pay themselves a reasonable salary, which is at least what other businesses would pay for similar services.

You also can avoid Social Security and Medicare taxes by keeping your business earnings in the corporation. The owners have to pay personal income tax on the amount they retain, but they would not have to pay Social Security or Medicare taxes. If you do take advantage of this, though, do not expect your Social Security benefits to be very high when you retire, because these are based on your contributions. You can offset this loss by planning for your own retirement by saving money in a tax-advantaged retirement plan, such as an IRA. You would probably make more from your own contributions than you would from Social Security. These plans are also tax deductible and only require that you wait until six months before your 60th birthday to take out money. You cannot collect Social Security until you are 62.

In order to be able to elect S corporation status, there are several restrictions that you must adhere to, including the following:

- You can have no more than 100 shareholders.

- None of the shareholders can be nonresident aliens (non-citizens who do not reside in the United States).

- You are limited to one class of stock.

- Shareholders can only be individuals, estates, or certain trusts. An S corporation cannot have a corporation as a shareholder.

If you are a one-person business and you are the only shareholder, these restrictions do not apply to you.

To establish your business as an S corporation, you must first form a C corporation and file an IRS Form 2553 to elect S corporation status. If you want to start off as an S corporation, you have to file the form within 75 days from the start of the tax year for your business.

You also should check with the appropriate state agencies to determine how an S corporation files and pays state taxes, if required. States tend to impose a minimum annual corporate tax or franchise fee. You can also face a state corporation tax on S corporation income. California, for example, imposes a 1.5 percent tax on S corporation profits to a minimum of $800. You are able to deduct state and local taxes from your federal income tax as business expenses.

Disadvantages to Corporations

There are a few disadvantages that come with incorporating. You will have to pay some taxes and fees that you would not have to pay as a different business entity. You also will have to maintain some minimal formalities. For example, the IRS and state corporation laws require that you hold annual shareholder meetings and document all important decisions through corporate minutes, resolutions, or written consents that have been signed by directors or shareholders. If you are the only shareholder or you only have a few shareholders, this is not a big deal. If you are large, this process can take some time. As a small business, you are able to prepare minutes that took place on paper only. If you do not comply with such formalities, you may suffer consequences. The IRS may fine you, you may lose tax benefits, and you may have to pay hefty fines. You can lose your corporation status because your corporation is considered false.

As a corporation, you are also required to keep a more complex bookkeeping system. You are required to have a corporate bank account, and you will need a more complex set of books. You also will have to file two returns, one for yourself and one for the corporation. It is wise to use the services of an accountant or a bookkeeper when you are first starting, particularly if you decide to form a corporation. Such a professional will be able to help you set up an appropriate system and will provide you guidance on your tax payments, tax deductions, and tax returns.

There are also some fees and taxes that you are required to pay as a corporation. If you are the employee of a corporation, you will have to contribute to unemployment compensation for yourself, a cost that will vary depending on your state of residence. You also will have to pay a fee to the state to form the corporation throughout its existence. The fee varies from state to state and is often between $100 and $300.

Creating a Corporation

To create a corporation, you have to file the necessary forms and pay the required fees to your Secretary of State or corporations commissioner. You also have to choose a name, adopt corporate bylaws, issue stock, and set up corporate records. It sounds complicated, but there are several preprinted documents that are available for you to use.

You may be required to sign a special form designating your corporation as a "professional" or "professional service" entity if you are involved in specific professions that have qualified you to be a PSC or PC.

A PSC or PC corporation must be organized for the sole purpose of providing services. All shareholders must be licensed to provide these services. If you have a medical corporation, all shareholders must be licensed physicians.

You are also required to use special forms and procedures to establish that you are a professional corporation, which means you might have to obtain a certificate of registration for the government agency that regulates your profession. The language of the profession may need to be included in your articles of incorporation.

There are also limits on the limited liability of a professional. Your limited liability cannot be used to avoid personal liability for malpractice or negligence that is due to your failure to provide a reasonable amount of care while performing your work or services. These businesses may be able to obtain additional business insurance to protect you against these risks, but these policies are often expensive.

Many professionals, particularly health care providers, carry malpractice insurance. If you are in a profession that is often sued for malpractice, you will need to investigate malpractice carriers and purchase insurance before you begin working in your professional capacity.

While this discussion of legal forms of business might have seemed overwhelming, it is important to remember that you can start your business as a sole proprietor very quickly and simply. Then, later, when your income begins to grow, you can talk to a tax accountant or attorney and decide to form an LLC or one of the corporate forms.

chapter 3

Naming Your Business and Writing Your Business Plan

Choosing a name for your business is one of the most important decisions you are going to make. Ultimately, your business name could very well mean the difference between success and failure. A business name is *that* important.

Take time to think about your business name and what you want it to convey. Do not go with the first decent name that occurs to you. It is better to create a list of potential names and choose from them.

Many self-employed individuals prefer to use their own name in their business name. For example, Joe Friday may be a private investigator who decides to name his business Joe Friday's Private Investigations.

If you are one of those entrepreneurs who would rather create a unique name, start the process with a brainstorming session. You might want to invite your family and friends to join in the process.

As you brainstorm names, keep the following tips in mind:

- Your business name should be meaningful and capture the key elements of your business.

- Your business name should be easy to pronounce and understand.

- Your business name should grab people's attention.

- Your business name should be spelled like it sounds, so it is easy for people to write it when you say it and easy for them to pronounce.

- Your business name must be easy to remember.

Legal Name

The legal name is the official name of your business. If you are a sole proprietor, your legal name is your name. It is also the name you always must use to sign legal documents, file tax returns, sign leases, apply for bank loans, and file lawsuits. You can use a form of your name, as in Joe Friday's example above, but you should not deviate too far away from your name, unless you decide to file a DBA, as described in the previous chapter.

The legal name you choose depends on your business entity. The vast majority of self-employed people are sole proprietors, so their legal name is their personal name.

If you form a partnership, however, using your legal name becomes much more difficult. With a partnership, you can use the last names of all the partners, or you and your partner can decide on a unique name as your legal name. If you want to use something other than your last names, you must draft and sign a written partnership agreement that includes the legal name. Should you choose the option to use an original name, you must ensure that you do not have the same name as another company. You must also register the partnership's legal name with your state.

If you create a corporation or an LLC, you also must choose a legal name for your business. Corporations, in particular, are required to have unique names. Once you have chosen your name, you must register it with the appropriate state agency, which, in most states, is the Secretary of State's office.

Trade Name

The trade name is the name you use to identify your business. It is also the name you will put on your business cards, stationery, marketing materials, and such. Your trade name can be your legal name, but it does not have to be.

Your trade name is the name by which the public will know you. After you choose a legal name, you then must decide whether or not you want to use it as a trade name. The simplest thing to do is to use your legal name as the trade name. Many sole proprietors will use a different trade name because their legal name is their personal name.

You may use your legal name as your trade name, but you are also allowed to add words to make it clear what type of business you are. For example, if you are a building contractor, your trade name could be "Jones Construction." You are not required to add anything to your legal name, but adding a description (i.e. Jones Construction) will give prospective customers an idea of what your business does.

Depending on where you live, you may or may not have to register your trade name with the state. Check with your Secretary of the State's office to determine if you are required to register your name. No matter where you live, you will always have to register the name if it implies that there is more than one owner, such as "Jones and Company."

You always have the option of making up a new name as your trade name. Many people prefer to create unique names because they are easier to market than a personal name. A made-up name is often catchier and identifies what your business does.

Your trade name can also establish you as an independent contractor. Employees do not use business names, so you can avoid problems with potential employer-employee relationship disputes. Additionally, you can obtain a bank account in your new name if you file a fictitious business name statement. To avoid confusion, you must provide your trade name along with your legal name when you file lawsuits, apply for loans, and conduct other business transactions.

Regardless of whether or not your trade name is your legal name, the name must be different than that of any other business in your field. If your name is similar to a name that is already being used in your industry, you may lose business because customers can get confused between the two businesses. You also could be sued under state and federal laws for unfair competition. Should you be sued and lose, you would be required to change your business's name and possibly face monetary compensation for damages.

The concern about similar names of businesses is most important within the geographic area where you are doing business. If you are doing business within one city, for example, make sure there is no other business in your city that has a name similar to yours. If you are doing business within a whole state, your search for similar names will have to be wider. Conduct a search to determine if the name is already in use or if there is a similar business name in your industry before you become set on a trade name. Names that are used in other industries that are totally unrelated to yours are often acceptable. Avoid using high-profile names such as McDonald's, even if your last name is McDonald. Believe it or not, some large companies sue to prevent small local companies from using their names.

To do a name search, go online and conduct a search. You also can check telephone books and business directories. You also want to find out if there are any similar, federally registered trademarks by using the U.S. Patent and Trademark Office's Web search at **www.uspto.gov**. You also can check Web hosting companies' Web sites to see if your desired name is available as a domain name.

As described in the preceding chapter, most states will require you to register the trade name under a "fictitious business name" or "doing business as" name. A sole proprietorship or partnership that is using a name other than the proprietors' personal names is considered "fictitious." A name that includes the words *company*, *associates*, and *sons* or *brothers* must also be registered because of the implication that there is more than one owner.

If you do not register your business name, you will not be able to open a bank account in the name of your business. You may also not be allowed to sue on a contract if you signed using the business's name.

There is often a time limit, usually within one to two months, during which you need to register. To register you will have to file a certificate with the county clerk, who generally is located at the county courthouse. The registration certificate states who is doing business and under what name. In some states, you also may be required to publish a statement in the local newspaper to allow creditors to identify who is behind the business name.

A small fee, generally ranging anywhere from $15 to $50, is required to register a business name. Additionally, the applicant has to fill out a short, simple form. Before you register your name, however, make sure you determine if anyone in your county is using the same or a similar name.

Naming a Corporation or Limited Liability Company

Naming a corporation or a limited liability company is different, as we already have discussed, than naming a sole proprietorship or a partnership. If you form a corporation or an LLC, you must get permission to use your corporate name by registering it with your Secretary of State.

To register a corporate name, you must do the following three things:

Step 1: Select a Permissible Name

Most states require that a corporation or an LLC use "corporation," "incorporated," "company," or "limited" in the business name. The only exceptions to the rule are Maine, Nevada, and Wyoming. The required descriptions can, however, be used as abbreviations. For example, you may run a limited liability company called Professional Writing. You can identify the company as a limited liability company by calling it Professional Writing LLC, if you wish.

Several states require names to be in English or Roman characters. Check with your Secretary of State's office to determine the particular requirements for your state. To find your Secretary of State's office online, simply go to any search engine and plug in the words "Secretary of State" and your state.

Step 2: Register Your Name

You must make sure that the corporate name is distinguishable from a corporate name already registered in the state. The state will not register a name that is too similar to names that are already on file. The Secretary of State or filing agency will search for similar names for you. Or you generally can check the availability of names by using the Secretary of State's Web site or office.

Step 3: Reserve Your Corporate Name

A corporation can reserve a name before incorporating if the name otherwise qualifies for registration. By registering your name before you incorporate, you protect yourself from having another business grabbing it before you have a chance to incorporate. Business names are held for 120 days, and most states allow for extensions if needed.

To reserve your corporate name, you first will have to submit an application for reservation, along with the required fee, to your Secretary of State. Some states also allow business owners to reserve corporate names online or over the phone. To determine the process in your state, check online or by phone with your Secretary of State's office or your state's corporate commissioner's office.

The process of registering a limited liability company is similar to that of registering a corporate name. Again, you must choose a name that adheres to your state's requirements. The business name also must denote that the business is a limited liability company by using the words "Limited Liability Company," "Limited Company," "LLC," or "LC."

Before you can register the business name, you must ensure that there is no other business in the state using the same or a similar business name. Again, to do this, simply call the Secretary of State's office. Do not forget that some states allow business owners to determine if their chosen business name is available on the Secretary of State's Web site.

States often will allow you to reserve your name for a period of 30 to 120 days. The registration fee is no more than $50.

The Legal Effect of a Registered Name

After registering their business names, many people mistakenly believe they are compliant with all the registration requirements of their trade name and that they have the right to use the name for all purposes. Unfortunately, this is not always the case.

Registering a corporate name, an LLC name, or even a trade name by filing a fictitious business name or DBA does not mean that you have a registered trademark. Registering your business's name simply allows you to do business under that name. It does not give you ownership of the name. If someone else uses the same name to identify a product or service, he or she may have it trademarked and thus will retain exclusive rights to that name.

If you use the trademarked name publicly, including on marketing materials, you may risk infringing on the existing trademark or service mark. If you have registered a name that was already in use or that is federally registered as a trademark, you will have to limit your use of the name to your personal checking account and check writing. If you plan to use your name on marketing materials, you must make sure that no one is already using the name.

This concept applies to the Internet as well. If you plan to market goods or services on the Internet, you must check to determine if the domain name is already in use. If it is, you will have to use a slightly modified name.

Choosing and Using a Trademark

By definition, a trademark is a distinctive word, phrase, logo, or other graphic symbol that you use to distinguish yourself in the marketplace. A service mark is similar to a trademark except a service mark promotes a service instead of a product. "Trademark" also refers to a generic term that is used to describe the entire body of state and federal law that regulates how businesses distinguish their services and products from their competition. Each state has its own set of laws as to when and how a trademark can be protected. The Lanham Act (15 U.S.C. 1050) is a federal trademark law that applies to all 50 states. You can find the full Lanham Act online at **www.bitlaw.com/source/15usc/**.

If you operate within a single state, your state laws cover you in the event that you are subject to a claim of trademark infringement. If you do business outside your state, you may be covered by both federal and state laws.

Your trade name should not be mistaken for a trademark or service mark. Trademark law does not protect your trade name unless you have used it to identify a particular product or service that you sell to the public. Businesses often will use abbreviations or shortened versions of their trade names as trademarks. Apple, for example, is a shortened version of Apple Computer Corporation, and "Apple" is used as the trademark.

A trade name is a trademark when it is used in a way that creates a separate commercial impression, such as when the trade name acts to identify a product or a service. The question of whether a product or service has created a separate commercial impression can be difficult to determine because companies will often use trade names and/or service marks on letterheads, advertising materials, signs, and displays. There are two general rules used to determine if the trade name is actually a trademark:

1. If the name is used in conjunction with contact information, it is probably a trade name.

2. If it appears to be a shortened version of the trade name, especially if there is a design or logo associated with it, the trade name is a trademark.

Unfortunately, not all trademarks are equal in the eyes of the law. A trademark should be distinctive, should stand out in the customer's mind, and should be easy to remember.

The more distinctive the trademark is, the more legal protection it will receive. A "weak" trademark will not receive much protection. Examples of a distinctive trademark include "Kodak" and "Xerox." Both trademarks are arbitrary, coined names.

To start the process of selecting a trademark or service mark, have a brainstorming session. When you have several promising ideas, begin market research to see how the potential marks appear to others, including potential customers, and to determine whether your chosen marks are already in use.

If you use all or part of your business name in the trademark or service mark, consider registering it as a trademark. Trademark registration is not required, but it is a good idea. It will make it easier for you to protect your trademark from people who may copy it, and it will put a notice out that the trademark is already taken.

If you only do business in your state, register the trademark with your state's trademark office. Most local businesses that do not do business in other states will fall into this category.

If you do business in multiple states, you should register your trademark or service mark with the U.S. Patent and Trademark Office. Registering a trademark or service mark requires you to fill out an application and pay a fee.

You also must be prepared to work with your state and federal trademark officials to get your trademark or service mark approved. Visit the USPTO Web site for more information about trademarks and trademark registration at **www.uspto.gov.** You can also register the trademark or service mark online using the Trademark Electronic Application System (TEAS). The TEAS allows you to fill out the application online and check it for completeness. You then can submit the form electronically.

The owner of the trademark that has been registered with the U.S. Patent and Trademark Office is entitled to use the special trademark symbol with the trademark, which notifies people that your trademark is registered. Using a trademark symbol is not mandatory, but it does make it easier for you to collect damages if someone uses your trademark.

Using a trademark symbol also discourages people from using the trademark. You can use an "R" or ® for trademarks registered with the USPTO, or you can use "TM" or ™ for trademarks that are registered with the state in which you are located. You can also use "Reg. U.S. Pat. & T.M. Off." if the trademark is registered with the USPTO. The use of the "TM" or ™ indicates that the trademark is being applied for. Only trademarks that have passed all the requirements of the USPTO may use the ® designation.

Depending on the strength of the trademark and whether you have registered it, you may be able to bring court action if others are using a similar or the same trademark. Trademark infringement occurs when the infringer uses a mark that is similar to yours and that can be easily confusing to consumers. A mark is not allowed to be identical to one already in use. If a proposed mark is similar enough to your mark, there is the risk of confusing consumers and the use likely will be deemed infringement.

Choosing Internet Domain Names

Unlike a decade ago, the vast majority of businesses and homes now have Internet access. In business, a Web site is essential to marketing and to staying in touch with Internet-savvy consumers. While a Web site certainly is not required to effectively run a business, it is fast becoming a necessity for businesses and the self-employed who want to stay competitive.

Let us assume that you are planning to design or have a Web site designed. The first step in the process is finding an Internet domain name. A domain name is simply your Web site's address on the Internet. For example, the Small Business Administration's Web site – with which you should become extremely familiar as a self-employed individual – is **www.sba.gov**. (The extension .gov is used for government organizations.)

There are three components to a Web site address. First, you have "www," the abbreviation for World Wide Web. Second is your domain name. You may use your business name for your domain name, if it is available. Third is the extension, as we previously mentioned. The most common extensions are .com, .net, and .org.

Internet users are generally most familiar with .com. Therefore, if you can snag a .com domain name, your best bet is to do so. (Some businesses purchase the .com in addition to other extensions, including .org and .net to ensure that: 1. the competition does not take the other versions of the domain name, and 2. your customers and prospective customers can find you easily, even if they type in the wrong extension.)

Unlike in the real world, it is impossible for two businesses to have the same domain name ending with the same extension. If someone is already using your business name as a .com, you will have to decide whether you want to use your business name with another extension or if you want to create a different version of your name.

There are two simple ways to determine if the domain name you want is taken. First, just go to your Web browser and type the name into your address bar. If a Web site appears or if there is a parked page, you know that the domain is already taken. However, never count on this method to determine if a domain name is available.

The second and best way to determine if your domain name is in use is to go to any Web hosting company (Domain Monger, for example, at **www .domainmonger.com**) and use the domain search function to determine if the name you want is taken. The search will tell you what extensions are and are not available for your domain name. For example, the .com may be taken, but the .net and .org may be available.

Remember, your goal is to choose a domain name that is similar to your business's name. But your domain name also must be easy to remember. If the domain name you want is already taken, you still might have a chance of snagging it. To find out who owns the domain name, go to WHOIS at **www.whois.net**. If the domain owner does not have a private registration (meaning he or she paid more to keep private details, including name and address, private), you will be able to get the information you need to contact the owner.

If the site is already live, you may just want to e-mail the owner to determine if he or she is willing to sell the domain name and at what price. You may find a domain owner who is willing to sell the domain name, but be prepared. Some domain names sell for hundreds if not thousands of dollars.

Once you register your domain name, no one else can use it, provided you continue to pay the registration fee every year. Most Web hosting companies offer domain registration when you purchase hosting. You should never purchase your domain name from your Web host unless you are 100 percent certain that you, not the Web hosting company, will own the domain name.

As a rule of thumb, you should always confirm that you will be the registrant and owner of the domain name before you purchase a domain name from a particular company. If the company is going to be the registrant and owner, find another company from which to purchase the domain name.

When a company owns your domain name, it can raise the price of registration considerably every year, and you will have no recourse. You will have to either pay the registration fee or find a new domain name. So, always make sure that you will be the registrant and owner of the domain name.

Following are several companies that sell domain names to help you get started:

- Domain Monger (**www.domainmonger.com**)

- Register.Com (**www.register.com**)

- Go Daddy (**www.godaddy.com**)

- Domain Bank, Inc. (**www.domainbank.net**)

- Yahoo Domains (**http://smallbusiness.yahoo.com/domains/**)

- Google Domains (**http://www.google.com/a/**)

Remember, do not let your registration lag, or another business can easily grab your domain name. The good news is most companies send out renewal programs, advising you of the date that your domain name registration expires, and some companies also allow for automatic renewal. If you opt for automatic renewal, remember to keep your credit card information current.

When you register your domain name, you have the choice of having your contact information (such as name, address, phone number, fax, and e-mail address) become public information, or you can pay a fee to have it remain private.

Domain registration is affordable and only costs between $10 and $20 a year. If you are sure you want to keep your domain name for a long time, you can register for multiple years right away and save on the yearly fee.

Your Business Plan

A business plan is essential to your success as a self-employed individual. Keep that old saying in mind: "If you fail to plan, you plan to fail." A business plan is your road map to success. In short, your business plan will define your business, business goals, marketing strategy, public relations and advertising goals, and how you are going to manage your business on a day-to-day basis.

A business plan is more than a map of where you plan to take the business. It is also a necessity if you decide to seek funding. Banks and other lenders will want to see a well-thought-out, clearly written business plan that gives them an overall picture of your business.

Other reasons to prepare a business plan are to make potential investors and advisors aware of your plans for your business and to motivate potential employees to join your company.

Even if you never needed money for your business, you should still prepare a business plan and keep it updated as your business changes.

Your Blueprint to Success

Because your business plan is the blueprint for your business, you must keep it current. Set aside time every six to 12 months, or as frequently as needed, to update your business plan. The good news is writing a business plan, while time consuming, is not particularly difficult. You can find a sample of a business plan on the accompanying CD-ROM or by doing an Internet search for "sample business plans." The following outline and in-depth detailed descriptions also will help you as you prepare to write your business plan.

Your business plan should be written in a concise manner and should contain as much information about your business as possible. As you write, you probably will notice that the information in your business plan becomes redundant. Remember to answer the questions: Who? What? When? Where? Why? How? How much? If you answer each of these questions concisely in one paragraph at the beginning of each section of your business plan, you will have something to expand on throughout the rest of the section.

There is no set size or length to a business plan. Often, businesses have business plans that run from 30 to 40 pages, but a plan for a simple business in which you are the only person and which is providing services may be as short as 10 to 20 pages. Your business plan also will include supporting documents, including research, demographics, and various other information.

Writing a business plan may seem like somewhat of a daunting task if you have never done it before. But, rest assured, if you follow an outline (you can use the one in this chapter) and set deadlines, you should have very few, if any, problems. Consider giving yourself a deadline for each section of the business plan and then set aside blocks of time to work on the business plan, as you may need to visit the library and other offices to gather the required information.

You can find a lot of the information and the demographics you need on the Internet. (Remember, however, that you should make sure you double check the information you find online to ensure accuracy of facts.) Save all your supporting documents and keep them organized so you will have an easier time when you are ready to sit down and write your business plan.

Getting Help Writing Your Business Plan

If the process of writing a business plan seems overwhelming to you, be aware that you do not have to do it all alone. There are several organizations that can help you with the details of the business plan and the startup of your business.

The Small Business Administration (SBA) is most commonly known for providing guarantees for small business loans, but this organization also helps new business owners with business plan writing and startup. The SBA has a wealth of information on its Web site (**www.sba.gov**), and local chapters offer workshops on small business each year. Check the SBA Web site for the location of the SBA office closest to you.

An organization affiliated with the SBA is the Service Corps of Retired Executives (SCORE). This volunteer group provides individual counseling and advice to new businesses. Check the group's Web site (**www.score .org**) to find the local office, and then call for an appointment with a SCORE counselor.

A third source of advice and information is the network of Small Business Development Centers (SBDCs) throughout the United States. SBDCs are located at colleges and universities through a partnership with the SBA, and they also provide individual counseling and workshops for new business owners. You can find the list of SBDC locations through the SBA Web site.

Taking advantage of these free services can help you in the writing of your business plan, and counselors also will evaluate your chances of getting funding for your business.

The Business Plan Outline

You must include numerous key elements when you write a business plan. Following is the basic outline that your business plan should follow:

I.   Cover sheet

II. Statement of purpose

III. Executive summary

IV. Table of contents

   A. Your business

      a. Business description

      b. Marketing plan

      c. Analysis of competition

      d. Employees

      e. Business insurance

      f.   Financial data

B. Financial data

      a.   Loan applications

      b.   Needed equipment

      c.   Balance sheet

      d.   Profit analysis

      e.   Profit and loss statements:

         i.   Summary for the first three years

         ii. Month-by-month detail for the first year

         iii. Quarter-by-quarter detail for the following two years

         iv. Assumptions upon which projects were based

         v. Pro-forma cash flow

C. Supporting documents to bring when applying for a loan

      a. The principals' tax returns for the previous three years

      b. Your personal financial statement (You can find all the required forms at your bank.)

      c. A copy of your recent credit report, if you have one

      d. A copy of your business plan, required licenses, and any other relevant legal documents

      e. A copy of each principal's résumé

      f. A copy of the letter of intent from your product's suppliers, if applicable

Step-by-Step: Writing Your Business Plan

To effectively write a business plan, you must know what information must be included. Unfortunately, new and prospective independent contractors and business owners easily can overlook this essential and extremely important aspect of preparing to start a business. Failure to write a business plan now could have negative consequences in the future.

The first thing you want to do is divide your business plan into six sections:

1. The cover sheet

2. The executive summary

3. The business description

4. The marketing plan

5. The management plan

6. The financial management plan

As previously discussed, your business plan also is going to include your financial projects and any relevant supporting documents.

The Cover Sheet

Your business plan's first page will be the cover sheet. The cover sheet is also your title page, and it will contain the following information:

- Business name

- Business address

- Business phone number and area code

- Logo

- Names, titles, addresses, and phone numbers, with area codes, for all owners

- The month and year the plan was written and issued

- Name of the person who prepared the cover sheet

The Executive Summary

The first thing your prospective lenders, and anyone else who reads your business plan, are going to see is the executive summary. Some experts believe the executive summary should be the last part of the business plan you actually write. Other experts encourage you to set out a dynamic summary of your business and use that document to drive the main business plan. Your executive summary should be as succinct as possible, and you should try your best to ensure it does not exceed two pages.

The executive summary is the single most important aspect of your business plan. In addition to summarizing your business plan in a succinct manner, it educates those who read it about your plans for your business. Consider the executive summary as a separate document that can be taken out of the business plan and still completely explain, in capsule form, the basics of the business plan. Some lenders read only the executive summary, and you need to be sure they have all the information they require.

Your executive summary must include:

- A mission statement summarizing your plans for your self-employment/business

- Your business's start date

- Each owner's name, including his or her title

- The services or products you offer

- A brief explanation detailing how your services or products will meet a need or needs of your target market

- A concise description of your experience in the field, including why your service or product is unique

- Most important, a brief description of the funding you require and your expectations for paying it back through the income of the business

You also should include, of course, such vital information as your business name, business address, business telephone number, business fax number, and business e-mail address.

The executive summary may be the only document seen by some individuals, so put it together with this in mind. Carve out enough time so you can develop a concise, strong executive summary. Even if you do not need funding now, or if you do not plan on anyone looking at your business plan, still write it as though others will be reading it and judging whether your business is worth the risk.

Even if you do not foresee needing a business plan right now, write one anyway. You never know when the need may arise, and it is better to have one ready than to have to scrape together something at the last minute. As you move forward, remember that old saying, "If you fail to plan, you plan to fail."

The Business Description

The first section you likely will begin writing when you start your business plan is the business description. Your business description, like the rest of your business plan, should be thorough yet concise. As you write the business description, you will need to think about your business's primary focus. You may want to jot down notes before you write the business description itself.

Start working on the business description by answering the following questions: What service(s) or product(s) is your business going to offer? Who is your target market? How is your business different from the competition? (In other words, what gives you a USP – unique selling position?)

Remember, you are going to revise your business plan during the course of your business's life, so what you write now is not set in stone.

The business description should have three parts: a description of your business, a description of the service(s) or product(s) you offer, and the location of your business.

In the first section, in which you describe your business, explain each of the following:

1. **Licenses/permits**. Include all business licenses and permits you need to legally operate your business in your city and state.

2. **Location and description of office**. If you are planning on buying a building or leasing space, mention this. If you will be operating from your home, talk about how your home office will be set up. Of course, if you already have a location, include the address here and describe the size and configuration of the office (rooms, rest rooms, reception area, work areas).

3. **Type of business**. Mention the legal entity you have chosen for your business: sole proprietorship, partnership, limited liability company, S corporation, or C corporation.

4. **Service and/or product**. Describe the services and/or products you will be offering.

5. **Character of your business.** Is your business already established, or is it a startup?

6. **Why will your business make a profit?** You also will want to answer the question: What growth opportunities does your business have?

7. **Business start date.** When will you officially begin business?

8. **Experience.** What experience do you have in this industry that will help you gain clients and start making money quickly? What have you learned about starting and running a business? You can research self-employment and running your own business in a variety of ways. Talk to other self-employment individuals. Run an Internet search. Talk with counselors at the Small Business Administration (**www .sba.gov**) and SCORE (**www.score.org**).

9. Make sure your business description clearly explains how the services or products you are offering to your clients stand apart from the competition.

Finally, make sure your business description is focused. Anyone who reads your business description should know your goals and why you have started or are going to start your new business.

Product or Service

The next section of your business plan will discuss, in detail, your products or services. If you are producing a product, you must include information on the raw materials you will use, how much those materials cost, who your suppliers are, where they are located, and why you chose those suppliers.

You should include a breakdown of your costs and rate sheets to back up your information. Consider including alternate suppliers as well and how you would deal with changes relating to your suppliers.

Many lenders generally also want to see how you would react in worst-case scenarios. You may hope for the best and plan for the worst, but lenders often plan for the worst first. Lenders typically like to see how business owners have anticipated problems and how they plan to solve those problems.

By addressing potential problems and how you will solve them, you are showing both potential lenders and anyone who reads your business plan that you have given a lot of thought to your business plan and your business. Because some businesses fail as a result of becoming too successful too soon, lenders want to see a business owner's plan for continuing a business and how that person plans to keep the business running smoothly and planning to handle growth.

On the other hand, you also want to include a best-case scenario. If your business is extremely successful, consider including plans for potentially hiring employees, purchasing additional supplies, and handling the influx of business.

If you provide a service rather than a product, explain the service you offer and why you are able to provide it. Discuss how you provide the service, who does the work, and where the service is performed. Show those who read your business plan why your business is unique and what special offers you are able to provide. Do not forget to include your future plans.

Location

While location is essential to your marketing plan, you also need to address it in the business description. Address the location of your business by stating something simple like, "My business is housed in 500 square feet of space in my home (or workshop and so on). It is located at 1111 S. 11th Street, My Town, My State."

Then explain why the site was chosen and back up your information with a physical description of the site, as well as a copy of the lease agreement or other supporting documentation. Provide background information on the site choice and list other possible locations, if there are any. You also may include photos, layouts, and drawings.

Accounting

Accounting is required for all businesses, so you must discuss it in your business plan. Provide details on what accounting system you will use and why you chose that particular system.

You also will discuss what portion of recordkeeping you will do internally and what portion you will do externally, including who is responsible for your bookkeeping records and who in your business is able to interpret the financial statements that are going to be provided by your accountant. It is extremely important for you to show how the accounting will be handled and how you will implement changes to make the company more profitable.

In the accounting section, include information on how you will handle receipts from clients and how you will deal with those who do not pay you promptly. Since many a business has failed by not managing receivables, lenders like to see that you have a plan for collecting receivables owed to you and what you will do with those who refuse to pay.

Insurance

Regardless of whether you work at home or from a rented office, you must have insurance to protect your business and your business assets. Make sure you discuss the business insurance you plan to carry and why you have chosen that insurance. Include the type of coverage you have, the insurance carrier, and what time period it will cover. Make sure you keep this information current, modifying it as needed, throughout the life of your business.

If you are in a profession that requires malpractice insurance, describe your plans to purchase this type of insurance, including information about the limits of the coverage and the insurance carrier.

Security

You also must consider the security of your business. If you are going to have employees, how will you safeguard your assets? Many businesses fail because employees steal from the businesses themselves. If you work from home or a workshop, how will you protect your building and your assets?

The Marketing Plan

The success of your business depends largely on your marketing efforts. Without marketing, a business has very little chance of surviving. To effectively market your business, you must know your customers: what they expect from your business, their likes, their dislikes, and who they are (for example, your target market's age group, education, income, interests, and so on).

Your target market is a group of customers who have common characteristics that distinguish them from other customers in the marketplace. Identify those characteristics and explain how you performed your research. Be sure to include information on:

- Resources and results

- Target market demographics

- Where your customers live and shop

- Where they work

- How many of your products are owned within the area where you will be located

Back up this information with documents – such as questionnaires and test marketing results – from the U.S. Census Bureau. Keep this section focused, reasonable, and verifiable.

When you begin marketing your business, focus on targeting those clients who are most likely to purchase your service or product. As your business expands, you may find that your customer base grows to include people outside your target market. When you get to that point, consider adjusting your marketing plan to include your newest customers.

Your marketing plan, which is an extremely important component of your business plan, as you can already tell, will require research and careful thought. To begin developing your marketing plan, ask yourself the following questions:

- Who is your target market? In other words, who are your customers likely to be?

- Is your target market growing, or is it shrinking? Or is your target market steady overall?

- How are you going to promote your products or services?

- How will you hold, win, or increase your product's or service's market share?

- How are you going to price your products or services? What is your pricing strategy?

When you can answer these questions, you are ready to move on and to start thinking about your competition.

Competition

No matter what products or services you offer, you are going to have competition. Some businesses have far more competition than others, but the fact is every business has competition. Expect it and be ready for it.

You will have two types of competition: direct competition and indirect competition. Direct competition is a business that offers the same product or service and has the same target market as you. Indirect competition is a business that offers the same product or service but has a different target market; indirect competition also may target the same market but offer a slightly different product or service that could affect your business. Evaluate your direct and indirect competitors and how you are going to be different. Emphasize how you will appeal to your target market in a better way and how you are going to tap into those as-yet-untapped markets.

To make it easier to evaluate your direct and indirect competition, break it down by doing the following:

- Ask yourself what five businesses are your closest direct competitors. What five businesses are your closest indirect competitors?

- After you have identified those ten businesses, determine whether each business is declining, increasing, or holding steady.

- Evaluate the advertising means of those ten businesses and then create a list of everything you have learned from advertising the business's operations.

- Make a list of the ten businesses and identify the strengths and weaknesses of each.

- Identify how the products and/or services of each business are different from your product or service.

When potential lenders look at your competition section, they should easily be able to discern who your top ten (five direct and five indirect) competitors are, how much of the market each holds, and what products/ services each offers. Moreover, they will know exactly how you plan to compete and how your customers will be able to find and use your products or services.

Consider using a chart or a worksheet to organize the research on your competition to show what they offer versus what you offer. Include an analysis of this information with a plan for how you will enter the market. You also will include how much of the market your competition currently has and how you will appeal to the market.

You also might want to create folders on your computer, one for each of the ten businesses you have identified as your competition. Put all your research in the folders and keep them updated. You should always keep an eye on your competition to determine what means they are using to advertise and promote their products or service, how often they offer sales, and how their products or services are priced.

Again, if you simply compile research and forget about it, you are not going to benefit. You must review your research and add to it periodically. Go to your competitors' Web sites and ask yourself: Does the Web and sales content grab your attention? Is it concise and easy to understand? How does the competition announce sales? Do they announce it with pizzazz on the front page of the Web site, or is it simply next to the regular-price item or service?

Carve out time to really get to know your competition. When you understand who they are and how they operate, you will be much more effective at creating winning marketing, advertising, and public relation campaigns.

Finally, make it a habit to always back up your hard drive at least once a week. That way, if your hard drive crashes, you will have a copy of your research.

Finding Information on Your Competition

If you are wondering where to find information on your competition, the possible sources depend on the type of business you plan to start. For example, if you are a local business offering products or services in your city, the phone book is the best place to look for competitors. Check the Yellow Pages and pay attention to the advertisements your competitors place. What do these ads tell you about the specifics of the products or services your competitors are offering? Note these benefits and put them in your analysis table.

If your business operates on the Internet, doing a Web search for potential competitors is the easiest way to gather information. As is the case with local companies, spend time noting both the way these companies advertise and what specific features or benefits they are promoting.

Finally, if your business sells to a specific industry, you can check industry trade publications or other trade directories on the Internet or in your local public library. Again, noting how your competitors advertise is the best way to determine the niche each one has established, and this will help you figure out your place in this group.

Methods of Distribution

In the methods-of-distribution section, you will illustrate how you plan to transport your products or how you will provide your services. Your distribution method should be closely related to your target market. If you are offering a product, you must show the purchasing patterns of your customers.

You also must identify how your customers purchase their products or services. Do they order them through a catalog or from the Internet, or do they go to a local store? Back up this information with statistics, rate sheets, contracts, and other documents. If you are providing a service, discuss how you will provide the service. Will you make house calls? How do you plan to handle mileage and fuel costs? Explain your response time. Be certain to list the pros and cons of all your various methods of distribution. Keep in mind your worst-case scenarios and provide solutions to your problems.

Advertising and Public Relations

Advertising and public relations are crucial to your business's success. Never allow yourself to believe that your product or service is so superior that it easily will sell itself. That is simply not true. If you have that type of mindset, you are only setting yourself up for failure.

The good news is advertising and promotion do not have to cost you a lot of money, especially when you are just starting out. There are numerous free ways to advertise your products or services, including starting a blog, creating an online community, posting on message boards popular with your target market, and writing articles for your local newspaper. With some creativity, you will have myriad ways to advertise and promote your business.

Tailor your advertising and marketing specifically to your target market. In this section of the business plan, you will discuss how you will use advertising methods, such as television, radio stations, publications, and the Internet to spread the word about your business.

Create an advertising and public relations plan. Remember, you can promote your business both online and offline. As with your business plan, your advertising and promotional material should always be concise and descriptive. It should tell your customers what they can expect from your products or services.

Finally, the advertising and public relations section of your marketing plan should include an analysis of your competitor's advertising and marketing strategies and copies of promotional materials. Make sure you tell potential lenders how you will spend your advertising budget. Discuss why and how you chose those methods and how the message will reach your target market. Do not forget to mention when particular advertising campaigns will begin and how long they will last.

Make sure you take the time to think about your marketing plan because it is the backbone of your business.

CASE STUDY: KATHRYN HENDERSHOT-HURD

Kathryn Hendershot-Hurd has been self-employed in marketing and Web development for ten years. Since she works from home, her biggest challenges from the beginning have been time management and maintaining a separation of work and home. In the five years it took her to become profitable, she made many mistakes. She took on anyone, as many startup businesses do, and she tried to do too much herself instead of hiring help.

Hendershot-Hurd believes that, above all, you need self discipline to be successful in a small business. She lives in southeastern Florida about five miles from the ocean, and she says it would be easy to "declare every day a beach day." No killer tan for her, though; she has put work before beach in order to see her business succeed.

Here is her advice to you as you start your new business: Discover what you do not know before you make the jump. For example, look at the other jobs done by people around you in your company, because you will be doing them yourself or having to hire others to do them.

Even though working for herself has been difficult, the benefits are great. For example, Hendershot-Hurd can take off to see her son in a national competition, and she will be able to work from her laptop and not have to ask a boss for time off.

CASE STUDY: KATHRYN HENDERSHOT-HURD

In addition to her Web development services, Hendershot-Hurd is also a marketing consultant. She is the author of *Beyond the Niche: Essential Tools You Need to Create Marketing Messages that Deliver Results.*

Virtual Impax

Kathryn Hendershot-Hurd

P.O. Box 13073

Fort Pierce, FL 34979

Phone: 772-336-0441

Pricing and Sales

Pricing is critical to the ultimate success of any business. Quite simply, consumers want quality products and services at competitive prices. Your pricing will be determined through both market research and an analysis of your finances.

Start by studying your top ten competitors before you create your sales strategy to determine the type of sales strategy they are using. By researching your competition, you will be able to determine whether your prices are competitive for your target market.

Developing a pricing strategy requires you to consider several different factors, such as:

- Product's or service's cost

- Overhead costs

- Costs of materials

- Pricing below your competition

- Pricing above your competition

A basic marketing strategy is to base the price within a range from the price ceiling to the price floor. Your market will determine the price ceiling or the highest price they are willing to pay. Mention what the competition charges and how much business they are getting; you also want to discuss the high quality of your product or service and how much demand you expect for it.

The price floor will be determined by the lowest amount you can offer for you product or service. To come to a figure for the price floor, determine all your costs, including raw materials, overhead, shipping, and so forth. The difference between the price ceiling and the floor will allow you room to offer discounts, accept returns, and help you deal with any bad debts you may incur.

If you sell a product, include your product's design in your pricing strategy. A product's design is critical. If you have a good design that catches consumers' attention, you are more likely to sell more products. Remember the old cliché, "Never judge a book by its cover"? The truth is most consumers do judge products by their packaging.

To ensure your package design appeals to your target market, you must determine the most appealing sizes, color, shape, and copy on the package. You want your package to grab people's attention, but you must comply with the Fair Packaging and Labeling Act and guidelines set forth by the U.S. Food and Drug Administration.

In summary, be as thorough and succinct as possible when discussing your pricing strategy and include specific details as to why you chose a specific pricing strategy.

Positioning

Positioning is the predetermined perceived value of your product or service in the eyes of your consumer. Your positioning is largely determined by your promotional activities. The first step to positioning is to identify what your product or service offers that your competition does not offer. You then can focus on those qualities that make your product or service unique, thus positioning it so that customers and prospective customers will immediately recognize its benefits.

Location

While location is important to your business description, it is also an essential component of your marketing plan. Start by simply stating the address of your business and whether it is located in your home or in an outside office. For example, "My office consists of 500 square feet of space in my home, which is located at 1111 S. 11th Street, My Town, My State."

After you list the address, discuss why you chose the particular space for your office, including a physical description of your work area and a copy of your lease, if applicable. Make sure you also include why you chose the site and the other possible locations you considered, if applicable. You might want to include photos, drawings, and layouts.

Market Entry

Carefully think about the timing of your entry into the market. Your products and services must be available at just the right time and the right place. Deciding when to enter the market, in large part, will depend on your target market's readiness for your product or service, and on your organizational schedule.

How well consumers receive your product or service generally depends on the time of year, including the season, the holiday, and the month. The best times of year to mail flyers and catalogs to customers and prospective customers are early January and September. Unless you have a holiday-related product or service, you will want to avoid entering the market in November or December.

Trade journals and trade associations (see the Directory of Associations online at **www.marketingsource.com/associations/information.html**) can be beneficial in helping you plan for your market entry. Include your chosen market entry date and why you chose that date.

Industry Trends

Know the trends in your industry and how they will affect you. Will the trends help your business or hurt it? Keep up with your industry trends by reading trade journals.

When you update your business plan, ensure that you also add information about the latest trends, including new technology and changes in the marketplace, and cite industry reports. Also include how to adapt as the market changes.

The Management Plan

Working for yourself is often attractive because it allows you to be your own boss. You call the shots. You decide how your business is run. But remember that managing your business is going to require a lot of hard work, determination, the ability to make decisions, and the dedication to build your business.

Even if you do not have employees, you must have some management skills, because you will have to manage your business's finances, advertising, and everyday operations. The management plan will help you build the foundation your business needs to succeed.

Employees are often a necessity to effectively run a business. As you are working for yourself, you may not need to hire employees, at least not in the beginning. Let us assume, however, that you are going to be hiring employees at some point.

The key to hiring employees is to find people who are strong in areas where you are weak. For example, let us say you are not really strong with creating powerful, attention-grabbing advertising and promotional material. So, you decide to hire an advertising specialist who will take over your advertising while you concentrate on those areas of business that utilize your strengths.

The first step to hiring employees is identifying what skills you need but do not have. If you cannot learn the skills you need or you cannot do so quickly enough, consider hiring or outsourcing those tasks to someone who has them.

Hiring employees requires that you know how to manage them and how to treat them with respect by showing them they are valued members of your team. When treated well, employees can be invaluable in helping you develop new ideas. They also offer different points of view that can positively influence your business.

Writing your management plan requires that you answer the following questions:

- How do your business experience and your background benefit your business?

- What are your weaknesses?

- In what ways can you compensate for your weaknesses?

- If you need a management team, who is going to comprise that team?

- What are the strengths and weaknesses of each member of your management team?

- What responsibilities does your management team have?

- Do you have an employee handbook or other document that clearly details each management team member's responsibilities?

- Is your management team going to be an integral part of your business for the long term or only during the startup phase?

- Do you currently have any personnel needs? If you do, what are they?

- How will you hire and train employees?

- What type of compensation package will your employees receive?

- Will you offer your employees any benefits, such as health insurance?

While you may not hire employees in the early years of your business, you may come to a point where you need them. Or you may work for yourself for the rest of your career and never need or want to hire an employee. Regardless, it is important to know what to expect just in case you do decide to hire employees in the future.

The Financial Management Plan

The final section of your business plan is the financial management plan. If you want your business to become and remain profitable, you must have a strong financial management plan. If you want your business to become a success, you must be able to manage your finances.

Every year thousands of businesses, many with the potential for great success, shut down because their owners simply did not know how or were unable to manage the business's finances. To avoid such failure, you must create a sound financial management plan that will keep you on track and ensure you meet your financial obligations.

The first step in creating your financial management plan is to estimate your startup costs and your operating costs. When you determine these, you can better create a business budget.

Some of your startup costs will be one-time costs and may include (depending on what services or products you provide) computer equipment, business accounting software, high-speed Internet, insurance, licenses and permits, supplies, legal and professional fees, and advertising costs.

Your operating costs are recurring costs you will have to pay throughout the life of your business. Operating costs may include taxes, insurance, equipment, advertising, Web hosting, and high-speed Internet. In addition, you should include in your operating budget enough money to cover all your project expenses for at least the first six months of your business. That way, if you do not make a profit or you do not make enough money, you will have enough money to help tide you over.

In addition to your startup and operating costs, your financial management plan also must include financial records to show your business's previous (if applicable), current, and projected finances. In all likelihood, you will need to make several financial assumptions. The financial management plan will also consist of pro forma (i.e., projected) and actual financial statements, as well as the following:

- Application for loan funds

- Cash-flow statement (budget)

- Three-year projection

- Break-even analysis

- Actual performance statements:

  o Balance sheet

  o Income (profit and loss) statement

  o Loan application/financial history

You will begin your financial management plan with a summary of your financial needs, which you will have identified when you created your startup and operating budgets. Lenders and potential investors must know your business's financial requirements when they are considering loaning you money or investing in your business.

Identify which of the three types of capital (working capital, growth capital, and equity capital) you need, how much money you need for each, and what you will do with that money.

- **Working capital:** Working capital is used to meet your ever-changing cash requirements. You likely will be required to repay the loan with cash earned during your business's next full operating year. At the start of your business, you will need working capital to pay your business expenses while you build up your customer base and income levels.

- **Growth capital:** Growth capital is used to meet your business's needs and will be repaid with profits over a period of years. If you require growth capital, you must show how you will use the capital to increase profits enough to repay the loan within approximately seven years.

- **Equity capital:** Equity capital is used to meet your permanent needs. If you require equity capital, you must raise it from investors who are willing to risk their money in return for a combination of dividend returns, capital gains, or a share in your business.

Use of Funds

The next section in your financial management plan is the use of funds. If you are seeking funding, a potential lender will require you to provide a statement of how the borrowed money will be used. Therefore, you must thoroughly but concisely explain how you will use the funds and then back up your statements with supporting documents.

You must ensure your supporting documents are well-organized for anyone, including the loan officer who will inspect them. Failure to organize your documents could result in a lender denying your application simply because he or she could not find the required information.

Consider using a table of contents in your financial management plan (you also may want to use a table of contents for your full business plan). Placing tabs that identify the different sections is also an excellent means of keeping your business plan organized.

Cash-Flow Statement

Your cash-flow statement is essentially your budget; think of the cash flow statement as a representation of your business checking account and the changes in this account from month to month. Cash-flow statements are documents that project what your business plan means in terms of cash, as the cash flow statement shows both the inflow and the outflow of cash. The cash-flow statement is an important part of your business, as it helps with internal planning as your business grows.

If you already have been in business for some time, you likely will find it easy to put together actual figures of income and expenses. If you have not been in business, you will create your cash-flow statement based on assumptions from your research and from your projected expenses. Your profit at the end of the year should be a proper balance between cash inflow and outflow.

Your cash-flow statement should identify the following key points:

- When you expect to receive cash

- How much cash you will receive

- When you will spend the cash to pay debts and bills

- How much cash will be required to pay for expenses

These key points allow the manager to identify the sources of cash. For example, will your cash flow come from sales of products or sales of services? Or will you need to borrow this cash? Do not forget to consider accounts receivable and how long it may take a customer to pay. When you are making projections, you always should include a best-case and a worst-case scenario.

Your cash-flow statement will deal only with actual cash; it will not include depreciation and amortization. A cash-flow statement is generally prepared to match the fiscal year of the business. Additionally, you should prepare a monthly, quarterly, and yearly statement.

You also will want to create three different budgets:

- Cost of sales

- Fixed expenses

- Variable expenses

Fixed expenses include items that always will cost the same amount, such as rent, rental equipment, loan payments, and Internet service. Think of fixed expenses as those costs that you must continue to pay even if you do not have any customers or income. Variable expenses are items whose cost may change from month to month, such as office supplies, postage, and so on. These costs vary based on the volume of sales and the number of customers. If you have more customers, you will need more office supplies, for example.

Following is an online resource that offers blank cash-flow statements that require you only to fill in the blanks: the Free Library (at **www .thefreelibrary.com**). This site provides links to several sites with free cash-flow templates. You likely will find that, even if you are not good with numbers, such forms are extremely easy to use. Still, you may need additional help compiling your financial information. If that is the case, consult an accountant.

Three-Year Income Projection

Lenders want to know what the future holds for your business. After all, your business has to be successful, or you will not be able to pay your lenders back. Three-year projections are required at the very minimum. However, if you really want to impress a lender, create your projections for five or ten years down the line.

Your three-year income projection is a pro forma income statement. If you already have been in business for a period of time, you will have a better idea of what you can expect in three years. If you have not yet been in business, use your market research and industry trends to help you in making assumptions. Your three-year income projection will include only income and deductible expenses, while your cash-flow statement includes all incoming and outgoing cash.

A three-year income projection can cover various time periods. There are several different opinions as to what period of time should be used. Some lenders prefer monthly income projections while others prefer annual income projections. Before you create your income projections, talk with the lender to determine what time period he or she prefers.

You will find all the information you need for your three-year income projection in your cash-flow statement, sales forecasts, and budgets. Again, if your business is new, you will use business and marketing analyses to create your income projection. And, if you have an established business, you will use your financial statements to create your income projection.

One option your lender might find appealing is for you to create several versions of your projections, titling them "best case" and "worst case" scenarios. The best-case scenario would be your estimation of the highest possible sales volume over the next three years; the worst-case scenario would be an extremely low estimate of sales. You also can create an "expected" scenario somewhere in between. This kind of estimation can increase your credibility with a lender who is skeptical about the possibilities for your success.

The three-year income projection also must take into consideration any fluctuations that may occur. Therefore, you must anticipate additional costs, efficiency issues, changes in the market, industry trends, and other similar factors. Increases and decreases in income and expenses are realistic and to be expected, so potential lenders will want to see these projections.

Break-Even Analysis

Creating a break-even analysis will help you determine if your company's expenses will match your sales or service volume and whether you will make a profit or incur a loss. You can project your break-even point in a graph or a mathematical formula. Break-even points can be expressed in total dollars or revenue offset by total expenses in total units of production.

To find your break-even point, define your fixed costs and variable costs. Fixed costs, as described above, will not vary with sales or production. These costs often are called "overhead," because they are over your head whether or not you have any sales. Variable costs will vary in direct proportion to your sales or production: The more sales, the higher the cost. Variable costs also include the cost of goods sold, because these costs directly vary with the amounts of products you have sold.

You can find all the figures for your break-even point on your three-year income projection. Then, you simply have to plug the figures into your formula.

Mathematical formula:

- B-E point sales = fixed costs / [1- variable costs as percent of total sales]

- B-E point sales = volume of sales at break-even point

- Fixed costs = fixed expenses, depreciation, interest (those costs that do not vary with sales)

- Variable costs = cost of goods sold and expenses that vary with sales volume

- Sales revenues = income from sales of goods/services over a specified period of time

Example:

B-E point sales (S) = ?
Fixed costs = $30,000
Variable costs = $50,000
Sales revenues = $100,000

$$S \text{ (at break-even point)} = \frac{\$30,000}{1 - (\$50,000/\$100,000)}$$

$$S = \frac{\$30,000}{(1-0.50)}$$

$$S = \frac{\$30,000}{(0.50)}$$

$$(0.50)\,S = \$30,000$$

$$S = \$60,000$$
(break-even point in terms of revenue expenses))

Note that calculating the break-even point is difficult for a service business, because most costs are fixed and only a few costs vary by sales. In addition, service businesses do not have figures for the cost of goods sold. To calculate the break-even point for a service business, assume that all business expenses are fixed, so the break-even point will be the point at which all costs are covered.

For example, if your service business had monthly expenses of $50,000, only a few costs would be variable, so your break-even point would be at the $50,000 sales level.

Graphical Break-Even Point

You also can plot your break-even point on a graph. There are many spreadsheet programs, including Microsoft Excel, which allow you to create graphs and charts.

The point on the graph where your total-expenses line intersects with the total-sales-revenues line is your breakeven point.

Actual Performance Statement

The actual performance statement is a financial statement that reflects the past activity of your business. Again, if your business is new, you will not have a business history. As a result, your actual performance statement will comprise your projected statements and your personal financial history.

If you have an established business, your actual performance statement will include the following:

- Balance sheet

- Profit and loss statement (income statement)

- Business financial history or loan application

The balance sheet is prepared at the close of an accounting period and illustrates your business's financial position on a fixed date. Additionally, the balance sheet offers a good overview of your business's financial condition at a particular time. Regularly preparing a balance sheet will help you identify and analyze trends in the financial strength of your business. All your balance sheets will contain three sections:

- **Assets:** Anything of monetary value that your business owns

- **Liabilities:** Debts that are owed by the business

- **Net worth (capital):** An amount equal to the owner's equity

Your assets are divided into three sections:

- **Current assets:** Assets that may be turned into cash within one year of the date on your balance sheet

- **Long-term investments:** Stocks, bonds, and special savings accounts that are kept for at least one year

- **Fixed assets:** Assets your business owns that are not intended for sale, such as land, buildings, equipment, vehicles, and such

Your liabilities are divided into:

- **Current liabilities:** Obligations that are payable within one operating year

- **Long-liabilities:** Outstanding balance minus the current portion due (e.g., mortgage, vehicles, and so on)

Your net worth is documented by the legal structure of your business.

- **Sole proprietorship or partnership:** Each owner's original investment plus earnings after withdrawals

- **Corporation:** The sum of owners' or stockholders' contributions plus earnings after paying dividends

Your income statement, or profit and loss statement, is a statement that shows your business's financial activity within a tax year, and it provides a picture of your business at any given time. The income statement is a tool that assesses your business's weaknesses in operation and efficiency. Income statements also can be used to compare your business operating efficiency and profitability over several years.

The income statement will show where your money came from and where you spent it, and it should be created at the close of each business month. At the end of each month, the accounts in a ledger are balanced and closed. Balances from revenue accounts and expense accounts then should be transferred to your income statement. Your income statement will be in the following format:

- **Income**

    o   Net sales (gross sales returns and allowances)

    o   Cost of goods sold

    o   Gross profit (net sales costs of goods sold)

- **Expenses**

    o   Selling expenses (direct, controllable, variable)

    o   Administrative expenses (indirect, fixed, overhead)

- **Total expenses**

- **Income from operations**

    o   Other income (interest income)

    o   Other expenses (interest expense)

- **Net profit (loss) before income taxes**

- Income taxes (federal, state, self-employment)

- Net profit (loss) after income taxes

Business Financial History

The business financial history, a summary of your business's financial information from its birth, is the final financial statement in your business plan. If your business is new, you will use your estimated projections. If you are applying for a loan, provide the lender with your personal balance sheet to illustrate how you have handled your personal business. Your balance sheet then can be used to assess your new business's potential for success.

If you are using your business plan to apply for a loan, your financial history is the same as your loan application. When working on your financial management plan, you should create your business financial history last; however, you want to place it at the beginning of the financial section of your business plan. When you indicate that you are interested in procuring a loan, the lender will supply you with a loan application. Be certain that the information on your application is accurate and can be verified, if necessary.

As you write your business plan, you will realize why you want to write this section last. All the information you include will be drawn from the previous financial documents you created. To help in the creation of your financial history, you may want to use the following:

- **Assets, liabilities, and net worth:** You can find this information on your balance sheet. If your business is just starting, you will most likely not have a balance sheet prepared.

- **Contingent liabilities:** Contingent liabilities are the debts you will owe in the future. If you are starting a business and you are not buying an existing business, you should not have any contingent liabilities.

- **Inventory details:** Inventory details provide information on your inventory that is derived from an inventory record. The inventory details also should have a summary of inventory evaluation methods (as determined by your CPA) and current inventory policies (that is, how long you typically hold inventory).

- **Income statement:** An income statement is your revenue and expense information. Transfer this information from your most recent profit and loss statement if it is available.

- **Real estate holdings, stocks, and bonds:** You may need to go through investment records for complete information. This information should also be included in the business section of your business plan.

- **Sole proprietorship, partnership, or corporation information:** This information will vary depending on your legal structure. Your supporting documents must include the necessary information for the tax forms that you will need to fill out based on your legal structure. For a sole proprietorship, for example, you will need a copy of your last three years' Schedule C forms. For a corporation, a copy of your last three years' corporate income tax returns will be needed.

- **Audit information:** Include information about who audits your books and how often. Include when they were last audited.

- **Insurance coverage:** Provide information and the amounts of your different types of coverage, including any malpractice insurance, business property/casualty/liability insurance, and insurance on vehicles owned by the business.

The financial documents that we covered in this section should be sufficient for you and your potential lender. Some lenders may not require all these documents, while others may want to see additional documents. Discuss the financial statement requirements with your lender so that you can supply him or her with complete information. You will help push the process along by being prepared.

Supporting Documents

Your supporting documents include additional information that should be included in your financial management plan. These are the records that back up your statements and illustrate why you have made the decisions you have in your business plan.

As your write your business plan, make a list of all the supporting documents that will be needed for each section. If you are applying for a loan, be sure to include existing equipment purchase agreements or lease contracts.

Here is a list of some supporting documents you may want to include:

- Résumé

- Personal financial statement

- Credit reports

- Copies of leases

- Reference letters

- Contracts

- Miscellaneous documents:

    o   Location information

o Photos

o Logos

o Stationery

o Demographic studies

o Maps

o Area studies on crime rate

o Income

o Other

Printing Your Business Plan

You want your business plan to look professional and polished. Once you have written your business plan, put it aside for several days and then proofread it. Or have someone else proofread it for you. Nothing says amateur like error-ridden copy, grammatical errors, and glaring typos. Consider hiring someone to proofread your business plan.

The overall appearance of your business plan is also very important. Many businesses have their business plans professionally printed and bound. Your cover should be a professional blue, black, or brown. You can have your business plan printed and bound at a professional printing company, or you can take it to your local office supply store or copy company and have it printed and bound at a reasonable cost.

Most business plans average between 20 and 40 pages. Remember, your business plan should be thorough yet concise. It also should be easy for any potential lenders to find the information they need.

Your presentation should be professional and polished. The business plan does not have to be typeset, but make sure you print it at either normal or best quality (in a Microsoft Word document, for example). It should be clear and easy to read.

Consider including tabs identifying the different sections, so it will be easy for lenders and anyone else who reads your business plan to flip from section to section. Do not forget to number the pages of your business plan.

Include a table of contents at the beginning of your business plan, after your statement of purpose. Make sure your table of contents is detailed enough for readers to easily flip to the corresponding pages. The table of contents should, of course, also list your supporting documents.

Creating a table of contents in a Microsoft Word document is simple. Make sure you use headings (found under the formatting tab) for each section. Go to "Insert," "References," and then "Tables and Indexes." Then click on "Table of Contents." After you have created your table of contents, you can update it by right clicking anywhere on the table of contents and clicking on "Update Entire Table."

CASE STUDY: DR. MARC FRITZ

In April 2007, I purchased a chiropractic office in Garner, Iowa. Garner is a community of 3,000 people located in rural northern Iowa. It is a community that is heavily involved in farming and industrial occupations. It is a great place to live, work, and raise a family. My wife, Amanda, and I moved to Garner for the opportunity to become self-employed and provide chiropractic care to people in need of chiropractic services.

As a sophomore in high school, I knew I wanted to learn more about natural health care, and chiropractic is a leader in natural, alternative health care. One of the many advantages of becoming a chiropractor is the chance to work for yourself.

The challenges that I have faced since I began working for myself are getting to know the people in the community, delegating job responsibilities, my young age, running a successful office/business, and being a compassionate, caring, yet authoritative doctor.

CASE STUDY: DR. MARC FRITZ

The chiropractic office that I purchased was established by another doctor in August 2003. He had built an office building, provided parking, and established a client base. Since I began working at the office, we have not seen a decline in the billing or collections. The office has maintained a steady-to-gradual growth in revenue. The practice has added x-ray services to promote this growth. Another unique feature we offer is patient counseling and education on different aspects of their health care needs and goals.

The obstacles that I had to recognize and overcome in practice are staff-related issues, managing expenses, office equipment, advertising, patient education, patient care decisions, and fees.

The main characteristics a person must possess to succeed in self-employment are an outgoing personality; involvement in the community, school, and development programs; and personal organization and motivation.

I asked for advice from everyone that I talked to when I first started out as a self-employed person. I thoroughly researched the town, the practice, the community, the industry, etc. I talked with my wife, my parents, my friends, and my professors; hired an attorney and an accountant; and talked with other professionals.

The advice I would offer to other people who are considering leaving the regular nine-to-five occupation is self-evaluation. Are you willing and able to sacrifice time, energy, and money to make things happen? Are you okay with working long hours without receiving compensation or recognition for your efforts? Are you able to take time off when you need to, to regroup and rethink your intentions? Are you able to ask for help when you need it? Do you need the company benefits?

The risk is worth the reward if you enjoy what you are doing, but it takes time for it to happen. Self-employment offers numerous advantages, including setting your own hours and your own goals. You are able to spend your time doing what you truly enjoy.

Garner Chiropractic

Dr. Marc Fritz

chapter 4

Setting Up Shop

Unlike most employees, as a self-employed individual you have the choice of where you want to work. Do you prefer working from home? Or would you rather rent an outside office to separate your home and business lives?

While many self-employed people opt for working at home, there are advantages and disadvantages to working from home, just as there are pros and cons to leasing an outside office. Consider your options and weigh the pros and cons carefully to ensure you make the right decision for your needs.

There are basic legal restrictions on where you can work that apply, whether you work from home or in an outside office. The decision you make will determine whether you can deduct your office expenses; however, whether you work from home or a rented office, your taxes will be the same.

You may find that working from a home office is ideal now, but your business may grow or you eventually may decide that you want to make the transition from home office to outside leased office.

The Home Office

For those who are employed by other businesses, working from home often appears to be the perfect situation. The fact is, working from home is often the ideal choice for the self-employed. Your choice to work from home or not will depend on several things, including the type of business you run and your personality. Weighing the pros and cons of working from home and renting an office is your first step to making the best decision for your business.

The Advantages of Working From a Home Office

Save time and money. One of the biggest advantages of working from home is the fact that you will save time and money. Working from home means you no longer have to deal with the frustration of rush-hour traffic.

What is more, with the ever-increasing cost of gas, you will save a considerable amount of money every month by eliminating your daily commute.

Furthermore, you will save a good chunk of money every month because you do not have to rent outside office space. Keep in mind, however, that how much you will pay for an office rental largely depends on where you live. If you live in a small town, you may pay just a fraction of what you would if you lived in New York City. To determine how much office space rents for in your area, check out the real estate section in your Sunday newspaper. By working from a home office, however, you also will be able to save a considerable amount of money that you can then invest back into your business and even devote to the expansion your business.

Deduct business-related expenses. When you work from a home office, you will be able to deduct all your business-related expenses. (The same is true when you work from a leased office.) If a client requires that you work on the premises, offer to pay something for the workspace he or she provides you. By paying for the workspace, you will have an easier time keeping your IRS status as a self-employed individual rather than as an employee of the client.

Working from home also allows you to deduct the costs you incur when you drive to meet clients or you travel to other locations for business purposes.

If your home office meets the IRS's requirements, you also will be able to deduct your home office expenses, such as a portion of your home's rent or mortgage, your utilities, and other expenses. (We will discuss the requirements later in the book.) The home deduction is particularly valuable if you are a renter as it allows you to deduct a significant expense that is not generally allowed as a deductible on your personal income taxes.

Flexibility. Working from home provides you with more flexibility than you have in a normal nine-to-five job. You can work whatever hours you choose: If you are a night person, you can work at night. If you prefer the typical nine-to-five schedule, you can work from nine to five. You can work as many or as few hours per day as you like, as long as you get your work done.

You also will have more flexibility in your schedule. For example, if you want to pick your child up from school every day, you can. Your time is your own to divide between your work and your family as you see fit.

Goodbye office politics. One thing many people who are self-employed enjoy is the lack of office politics and gossip. When you work at home, you no longer have to worry about coworkers or a boss stopping by your desk for a chat that will eat into your work time.

Dress how you want. Unless you will be meeting with clients, you can dress however you want when you work: in your pajamas, in a T-shirt and jeans, or in a suit and tie. Working from home allows you to dress however you feel most comfortable, and it can save you money on an expensive wardrobe.

The Disadvantages of Working From a Home Office

While working from home may seem like paradise for some, there are disadvantages you should consider fully.

You must have discipline. Working from home requires that you have strict discipline. Even if your office is separated from the rest of your house, you are going to have distractions all around you. The television, the telephone, and your family are only a few of the distractions with which you must deal.

Your best bet is to set working hours, and tell your family and friends those are the hours during which you cannot receive phone calls, run errands, or be bothered unless it is an emergency. Setting office hours is often the ideal way to separate your work life from your home life while working in the home.

You may not be allowed to work from home. If you are not seeing customers, you probably can run your business from home, but there are some situations that do not allow people to work from home. For example, you may live in a community run by a homeowners' association that forbids people from running their businesses from home. Or you may live in a city that has so many restrictions that you simply cannot do it. In some cities, you may be able to poll your neighbors to see if they would allow you to operate from home. If no one objects, you may be able to get a variance from the city.

No more coworkers or bosses. If you are a sociable person, you may get lonely working by yourself from home. You no longer will have constant, daily interaction with coworkers or a boss, unless you grow your business to a point where you hire employees or independent contractors.

Appearances. Some professionals perceive working from a home office as unprofessional and, therefore, do not take those who work from home as seriously as they would someone working from a leased office.

While it is unfortunate that some have this view, you can portray professionalism in a number of easy, inexpensive ways, such as by having a phone line installed that is exclusively for your business. You can purchase an 800-number for a fairly low fee, if you want to offer clients the option of contacting you via a toll-free number. You also will have to consider how you are going to answer phones when you are not in your home office. You can have voicemail with a professional message, pick up all calls, or hire an answering service to take messages for you. Of course, you can have a devoted mobile phone for your business, instead.

Second, ensure all communication is on professional letterhead with matching envelopes. The good news is you do not have to spend a lot of money having letterhead professionally designed. You simply can purchase quality stock letterhead, with matching envelopes and business cards, at most office supply stores.

Third, consider renting a post office box. Some companies, like Mail Boxes Etc., offer boxes that give you a full address. For example, instead of your address reading P.O. Box 123, it would read like a normal street address, such as 123 My Street. In addition to giving an appearance of professionalism, a rented box also will ensure your business mail and private mail remains separate.

Finally, rather than using your own name (e.g., John Smith, professional printer) for your business name, create a separate business name, such as Professional Printers.

Security concerns. If you work from home, you will want to invest in insurance to protect your work equipment and your business, should disaster strike. You will not have the same protection you would have if you worked in an office building with security guards and/or security cameras.

When working from home, separate your business from your personal life as much as possible, taking precautions by using a post office box rather than your home address; not keeping large amounts of cash in your home office; and only holding meetings with those who make an appointment.

Use common sense when running your business from your home. Do not inform people when you will be out of the house for the day or gone on vacation. Instead, tell clients and prospective clients you will not be in the office. Do not give out too much information.

Businesses Conducive to Working From Home

There are some businesses that are better suited for a home office than others. Those businesses that are particularly conducive to a home office include:

- Writing
- Editing
- Graphic design
- Web design
- Consulting

- Telemarketing
- Accounting
- Photography
- Financial planning
- Music lessons

There are also businesses that you can run from your home office, but the work actually takes place outside your home. Such businesses may include:

- Catering
- Maid services

- Carpet cleaning
- Delivery service

- Home inspections
- Cleaning pools

- Carpet cleaning
- Pet sitting

- Construction
- Piano tuning

Of course, these are only partial lists of the many businesses that are conducive to working from home. Some businesses, by their very nature, will not be well-suited to a home office. For example, if you are a professional, like an attorney who meets with many clients on a daily basis, you probably will be better off working in a leased office. Having clients stream in and out of your house each day could aggravate your neighbors.

Additionally, if you hire employees, you likely will want to rent professional office space for two reasons. First, employees can require plenty of office space. Second, many cities do not allow employers to either have employees in a home office or have more than two employees working in a home office.

The Advantages of Working From a Leased Office

By now you probably have a pretty good idea of whether you want to work from home or from a leased office space. Both have their distinct advantages and disadvantages. The advantages of working from a leased office include:

Professional setting. Some clients and prospective clients may perceive you to be more professional by operating your business from a leased office. Additionally, you will be able to hold meetings and allow clients and prospective clients to visit your office without first having to make an appointment.

More efficient. If you are the kind of person who is easily distracted by the television or your family, you likely will find you get more work done at an office away from your home. Some people prefer keeping their work life separate from their private lives.

The Disadvantages of Working From a Leased Office

You cannot deduct certain expenses. Whereas you can deduct traveling expenses when you work from home, you cannot deduct the expenses you incur traveling to and from work every day.

High rental costs. Rental costs vary greatly from place to place. If you want to lease an office in a big city like New York City, you likely will pay much more per month than you would if you want to lease in a small town.

Less flexibility. When you work from home, you can work when you want and how you want. When you work from a leased office, you will have to dress in a more professional way, and you likely will have to set more traditional hours.

Tips for Leasing Office Space

Whether you decide leasing office space is right for you now or in the future, you should have an idea of what to expect and how to go about the process. Leasing office space is much different than leasing residential accommodation, so consult a professional commercial realtor to help you.

Is the office space appropriately zoned? One of the first questions you should ask is, Is the office space zoned for commercial purposes? Cities zone space in one of four ways: residentially, commercially, industrially, or a combination of the three. Make sure the office spaces you are considering are zoned for commercial purposes.

What space is included in the monthly rent? Commercial office space rent is determined by how much square footage the office contains. For example, if a landlord is charging $10 per square foot on 1,000 square feet of space, you would pay approximately $10,000 per year to rent that space.

Determine what is included in your rent. Are the bathrooms and hallways, which are used by everyone in the building, considered part of your rent? Know exactly what your rent covers.

What is the term of the lease? What is the duration of the lease? You will find that it is possible to negotiate the actual term of the lease anywhere from a month to several years. If this is your first time leasing office space, consider either a six- or 12-month contract. You also may want to negotiate with the landlord to allow you to renew your lease once the initial term has expired.

How much of a security deposit is required? As with residential space, you are going to have to pay a security deposit. Do not just agree to the security deposit with the landlord. Instead, negotiate for an amount that is fair to both of you.

Ensure you also get a concrete date as to when the landlord will return your security deposit. For example, if you move out of the office space after your lease runs out, when will the landlord return your security deposit? Consider also negotiating with your landlord to pay you part of your security deposit back, provided you pay your rent on time for a specific period of time.

Who is responsible for the maintenance of the office space? Someone has to maintain the office space, whether it is cleaning or repairs. Make sure the lease clearly states who is responsible for the maintenance of the office space.

Who is responsible for any improvements to the office space? If there are improvements to be made to the office space, who is responsible for making them? For example, let us say the office space needs new lighting. Will you or the landlord be responsible for purchasing, installing, and maintaining the new lighting? Make sure the lease clearly states who is responsible for improvements or modifications to the office space.

What if you want to terminate your lease early? People do not sign a lease with the intention of terminating it early. Yet, unexpected events can make this necessary, so make sure you know the consequences of termination.

There are two possible scenarios. First, your lease will state explicitly that you cannot break your lease. In such an instance, you are responsible to pay the rent until your lease expires. Second, you may be able to break your lease provided you pay a pre-determined fee to the landlord.

How often can your landlord increase your lease price? Commercial landlords increase rent by approximately 5 percent every year. The lease should include a price cap for how much a landlord can increase your rent annually.

Before you sign on the dotted line, have an attorney look over your lease to ensure everything is as it should be. Your lawyer will protect you and ensure that anything that unfairly favors the landlord is negotiated.

Home Office Deductions

When you work from a home office, you will benefit from numerous deductions as long as you keep good records of all your business-related expenses from the previous year. In addition to using an accounting system that will allow to you track all your business related expenses, you must keep all your receipts to ensure you get all the deductions you are allowed.

Among those expenses you will be able to deduct when you file your taxes are:

- Office supplies

- Business-related mileage

- Travel-related business expenses

- Your business's equipment, including your computer, photocopier, scanner, and fax machine

- A phone line, specifically for your business, and all related charges

- Business-related telephone calls made from your home phone

- Computer software

- Retirement contributions

- Health-related expenses, such as prescriptions and health insurance

Some of the expenses that are not tax deductible include:

- Your home telephone line

- Your wardrobe (unless you have to wear a uniform for your business)

- Traffic tickets

- Living expenses

- Family expenses

You can do one of two things if you are not sure if a particular expense is tax deductible. First, you can ask yourself the following questions:

• Did you pay for the service or product during the tax year?

• Are your expenses necessary according to the IRS?

• Are your expenses ordinary according to the IRS?

• Are the expenses related to the running of your business?

If, after answering those questions, you still are not sure, consult your accountant or tax professional. Or you can consult the IRS's Web site at **www.irs.gov/publications/p535/index.html**.

Equipment

Before you can begin your self-employed life, your home or leased office will have to have the equipment needed to run your business. The exact equipment you need will largely depend on your business. A writer is going to need far different tools than someone who runs a maid service. Still, as you will see, there are some pieces of equipment that most self-employed individuals are going to need.

Office Furniture

If you have a business which requires you to work in an office for any period of time, you will need office furniture, including a desk and a chair. Rather than spending money on brand new furniture, consider purchasing secondhand furniture. Be on the lookout for companies that are going out of business and that are selling their furniture.

Computer

If you do not have a computer, you can purchase one for $1,000 or less. If you are short on funds, you may want to consider purchasing a refurbished computer, which are just as good as new computers and cost a fraction of the price. Look in your local phone book for a computer company in your area.

Business Phone Line

A business phone line is a sign of your professionalism, and if you work from home, it will help separate your business from your home life. Shop around for phone providers. Some carriers offer bundled packages that offer such services as unlimited local and long-distance calling for one flat fee. If you take calls from around the country or the world, consider adding a toll-free line. You can obtain one for a low monthly cost from an Internet provider, and you might be able to get a memorable number for this purpose.

Internet Access

Having Internet access is rapidly becoming essential for business owners and self-employed individuals. Unless you live in a rural area where your only option is dial-up, consider using DSL, broadband, or cable Internet. It is much faster and will save you time.

Some telephone carriers and cable companies offer bundled packages that combine phone and Internet service, so be sure to shop around to find the best prices.

Computer Software

To keep track of your expenses and your income, you are likely going to need accounting software (which we will discuss in greater detail in Chapter 10). If you decide to design your own Web site, you may also need to purchase Web design software, such as Microsoft FrontPage or Adobe Dreamweaver.

Web Site

Regardless of what type of business you run, if you want to become and stay competitive, you need a Web site. Essentially, a Web site is your online business card. It is an easy way for prospective customers from around the world to learn about the services or products you offer.

The good news is, if funds are tight as you make the transition from employee to self-employed individual and you cannot yet hire a professional Web designer, you can create a Web site for very little. All you need is a Web design program (such as FrontPage or Dreamweaver) and a free template. Once you have a template, all you need to do is purchase a domain name and hosting service and add your content.

Consider creating a Web presence as soon as possible. Web sites are becoming a necessity for those who run a small business.

E-mail Address

To make it easier for clients to contact you, you need an e-mail address. It is not a good idea to use a free e-mail host, like Yahoo or Google, because you want to present professionalism. If you have a Web site, you can create your e-mail through it. For example, if your Web site is **www.janedoe.com**, you can create an e-mail address from your domain (i.e., **me@janedoe.com**).

How to Determine Operating Costs

Before you begin your life as a self-employed professional, you will need to create an operating budget to help determine how much money you need to successfully run your business. Do not put off creating your budget. Rather, face it head on before you open your doors for business.

There are two types of costs that are included in your budget: variable costs and fixed costs. Variable costs, which tend to occur once or just a few times, include items such as office furniture, a computer, and computer software. Fixed costs, on the other hand, are costs you have every month, such as utilities, telephone bills, and charges for Internet access.

Knowing what costs you will have every month is the first step in creating an effective budget. However, do not create your budget until you answer the following questions:

- How much money do you have?

- How much money will you need to effectively run your business?

- How much money will you need to purchase equipment?

- If you will be hiring employees or independent contractors, how much capital will you need so you can pay them?

- What is the total of all your startup costs?

- What are your expected profits on a monthly basis?

- What are your day-to-day costs?

- How much money must you make to keep your business running smoothly?

Be sure to answer each of these questions honestly and directly. Waiting to answer them until later is a recipe for disaster. By answering them now, you will better be able to determine if you can afford to hire employees, or if the office you are considering is within your budget, for example.

If you determine that you cannot yet afford everything you need or want for your business, be prepared to cut back. Instead of purchasing brand-new office furniture, for example, buy used. We discuss in depth the many ways you can save money later in the chapter.

The Small Business Administration advises that an operating budget should take into account such expenses as rent, depreciation, insurance, personnel, advertising and promotions, loan payments, accounting, legal, payroll, supplies, utilities, salaries, dues, fees, subscriptions, repairs, maintenance, and taxes (including local, state, and federal). Of course, some of these expenses – such as personnel and salaries – may not apply to you now, but perhaps they will in the future.

According to the Better Business Bureau, it is best to keep your budget simple. The organization recommends you only use two pieces of paper: one for your expenses and one for your income. On those two pieces of paper, write all your estimated (variable and fixed) expenses and income for the upcoming 12 months.

Beware of the critical mistakes business owners often make when creating a budget. First, be realistic. Of course, you want to be optimistic about success in your first year of business, but remember to be level-headed about your expected expenses and projected income.

Additionally, you must keep careful track of all the money that is coming into and going out of your business. (We will discuss accounting and bookkeeping methods in more detail in Chapter 10.)

Tips for Opening a Business Bank Account

Regardless of whether your business entity is a sole proprietorship or a corporation, you will need a separate business bank account for your business. Having a business bank account will benefit you and your business in several ways.

First, a business bank account is a sign of professionalism, signaling to others that you are serious about running your business in a professional manner. In the case of an IRS audit, the fact that you have a business bank account shows that you do not consider this business just a hobby.

Second, your business bank account will help you keep track of all the money that comes into and goes out of the business. Finally, a business bank account is an excellent way to verify each of your expenses and how much you paid for them every month.

Fortunately, opening a business bank account is straightforward and fairly simple. Start by researching the banks that offer business bank accounts in your area. When researching small-business bank account options, ask the following questions:

- Is online banking for small businesses available?

- Does the bank offer telephone banking?

- Can you log onto the Internet to access important information, such as your account balance, paid expenses, and whether checks have cleared? (Some banks allow customers to view canceled checks online.)

- Does the bank have branches nationwide?

- What, if any, fees are there for opening a small business account?

- What are the fees associated with maintaining a small-business account?

- For how long must you have an account with the bank before you can apply for loans or overdraft protection?

- Does the bank offer small-business credit cards? If so, how long must you be a customer to be eligible for the credit card? What are the terms of the credit card?

• If you need a loan in the future, how much does the bank generally lend to small-business owners? What is the typical interest rate and repayment schedule?

• Will you get a business debit card?

• Can you obtain online merchant services from this bank?

Some banks also allow business owners to open an account online. Regardless of whether you head to the local branch of your chosen bank or if you open your account online, you must be prepared. You will have to present documentation, including your EIN number. Before heading to the bank to open your small-business account, contact the bank to find out exactly what you need to present when applying for a small-business account.

Tips for Finding Financing to Fund Your New Business

Starting a new business, or making the transition from employee to self-employed professional, costs money, and you may not have enough funds to get your business off the ground. Fortunately, there are various sources of funding you can use to help start your business.

Savings. If you have money squirreled away for a rainy day, you may be able to dip into it to help cover your startup costs. However, before you make a withdrawal from your savings account, carefully consider whether you can afford to use your savings.

Most experts agree that leaving a cushion of at least $5,000 in a savings account is best. Draining your account, on the other hand, could be disastrous. You never know what emergency, business or personal, might occur, so leave as much as you can in your savings account.

You may also want to borrow against your retirement savings, such as a 401(k), if the funds are available. Before you borrow against any retirement savings, however, make sure you know exactly how much you are allowed to borrow, how long you have to repay the loan, if applicable, and the interest on the loan.

Friends and family. Are your family members or friends interested in lending you money to help fund your startup? You likely have heard the saying, "Never do business with family." To some extent, that is sage advice; however, family can sometimes offer important, even necessary, support to the self-employed professional.

If you are going to request a loan from your family or friends, make sure the whole transaction is done professionally. Have a contract drawn up, stating the terms of the loan (how much you are borrowing, how much interest you are paying, how long you have to pay it back) very clearly. Even if a loved one says he or she is giving you a loan with no strings attached, still write a contract.

One of your family members or friends might request, instead of you paying the loan back, that you simply allow them to become an investor in the business by issuing them stock. Consider such a request very carefully. If a loved one holds stock in your business, he or she effectively gets to have a say in how you run your business.

Partner/investor. If you are willing to allow someone else to have a say in the way you run your business, you may want to consider finding a partner or an investor. Again, make sure you do not mind relinquishing some control of your business to another person.

To find a suitable investor or partner for your business, start researching your options. Talk to your loved ones, coworkers, friends, and others to determine whether they know anyone who is interested in investing in a small startup.

Talk with your attorney, accountant, and any other professional with whom you deal. You never know who may be able to help you find the ideal investor for your business.

Your ideal investor should have particular expertise in your field and should be able to contribute to your business. Once you find an investor with whom you want to work, have your attorney draw up a contract that will define your business relationship.

Credit cards. If your credit cards offer a low interest rate, you may want to use them to help fund your startup. Some credit card companies offer customers cash advances. The upside to cash advances is that you can withdraw the money from an ATM. The downside to cash advances is the high interest rate that is often attached to them. Credit card companies can charge much higher interest rates for cash advances than for credit.

Bank loan. Consider applying for a bank loan. Be aware, however, that some banks require that your business has existed for a certain period of time before you are eligible for a bank loan.

The key to securing a bank loan that is best for your needs is to research your options. If you are not certain which banks have a strong reputation for offering business loans, talk with a business advisor at the SBA or ask others if they can recommend a lender. Always check a lender's reputation by visiting the Better Business Bureau's Web site at **www.bbb.org**. By doing a check, you can determine if there have been any complaints against the lender and how those complaints were resolved.

Talk with loan consultants at each of the banks with whom you are considering applying for a loan. Ask the loan consultant plenty of questions; for example, if you borrow this much money, what will your monthly payments be? What interest rate can you expect to pay? How long do you have to pay back the loan? Is there a penalty if you pay the loan off early?

Do not choose the first bank that approves you for a loan. Instead, take the time needed to research and choose the best loan for your needs. Never sign on the dotted line until you have an attorney review all the loan documents.

But do not just let your attorney read your loan documents. Make sure you read them carefully as well, making note of any questions you may have that you can ask your attorney or the lender.

SBA loan. The Small Business Administration is an extremely valuable organization for entrepreneurs and small-business owners, and as an entrepreneur, it is an organization with which you likely will become extremely familiar. In addition to providing valuable information and advice for small-business owners, the SBA runs several programs designed to provide loans to those small business owners and entrepreneurs who want to start or grow their business.

When you apply for an SBA loan, which is government-backed funding, you will not get the funds loan directly from the SBA. Rather, your loan will be issued by a designated bank or other financial institution. The SBA simply will act as the guarantor of the loan.

The good news about applying for an SBA loan is the fact that you do not have to have a high credit score. Even if your credit score is a bit low, you still may be eligible for a loan. SBA loans are particularly attractive to both lenders and entrepreneurs because the loans are backed by the government. To learn more about the different SBA loans available or to apply for an SBA loan, go to **www.sba.gov**, or contact your local SBA office for more information.

Cost Cutting Ideas

Regardless of whether you have unlimited resources or you are on a shoestring budget, you likely want to find ways to cut back on the costs of running your small business. Fortunately, there are numerous ways you can reduce your costs, including:

- **Buy used.** If you have to furnish your office, buy used furniture rather than brand-new furniture. You may save hundreds of dollars, especially considering that office furniture loses approximately 25 percent of its value the minute you take it out of the store.

- **Buy local.** If you need to purchase products (e.g., printer ink, office supplies, computer software, and the like), go to stores in your area rather than ordering online or from a catalog. That way you will save on shipping costs.

- **Buy in bulk.** Join Sam's Club, Costco, or whatever warehouse store is in your area, and purchase in bulk. You will save money and have enough of a supply to tide you over for quite some time.

- **Comparison shop.** Do not purchase the first product or service you research. For example, let us say you need a business telephone line, so you begin researching the telephone companies that offer service in your area. Choose the one with the best package for your needs. However, do not become complacent. Every so often (every six months or so), check to see if your current telephone carrier can offer you better rates. If it cannot, start shopping around for other carriers with better deals.

- **Negotiate.** If you are buying a product or a service, talk with the seller and try to negotiate a lower price. You might be surprised at how willing some people are to negotiate. Besides, someone saying no is the worst thing that can happen.

- **Attend trade shows** and purchase the products you need there. In many instances, vendors at trade shows offer attendees big discounts.

- **Do not buy brand names.** You do not need brand-name paper, pens, or other office supplies. You can save money by buying generic, store brand products. In many instances, those generic products are made by the same manufacturers as the brand-name products.

- **Shop around for insurance** on a yearly basis rather than allowing your insurance to automatically renew. It is common for people to pick an insurance company and stick with it. It is easy to get comfortable with your insurance, and it may be a bit of a hassle to switch insurance companies. However, if it saves you money, it is worth it.

- **Invest in a postage scale.** Purchasing a postage scale and ensuring that it is programmed with the correct postage rates can help you save significant money on your mailing costs.

- **Buy your business checks anywhere but the bank.** You can find a much better deal on business checks elsewhere. Look online for deals, or find a coupon in a local coupon book.

- **Request discounts.** If you consistently work with a vendor, ask if he will give you a discount if you pay your invoices with a check. Or ask if you can be given a discount if you make your payment before the due date.

- **Always pay your bills on time** to ensure you do not incur late penalties.

- **Reconsider the organizations of which you are a part**. Many self-employed people belong to industry associations. A writer, for example, may belong to the National Writers Union, the Chamber of Commerce, and several other writing industry associations. To what associations do you belong that require you to pay dues? Do you actively take part in those organizations, or do you benefit from them in some way? Or do you just write a check to cover the fees every year? If you answered yes to the latter, consider dropping out of those organizations.

Saving money and cutting costs while starting and running your small business is possible as long as you are vigilant in keeping track of the money you spend and make sure you only spend when it is necessary.

chapter 5

All the Proper Licenses, Permits, and Identification

All businesses are required to have the proper licenses and/or permits before they officially begin doing business. Often, you will have to pay a nominal fee to apply for the business licenses and permits you need. To determine exactly what business licenses and permits your city and state require, go to your city's Web site and the Web site for the Secretary of State in your state.

Following are some of the permits and licenses you likely will need before you open your doors for business.

Local Business Permit

Whether you are going to work from a home office or a leased office, you must apply for a local business permit with your city or town. Local business permits require that you pay a fee annually to keep the permit.

To determine exactly what business permits you need locally, contact your local city hall.

You may also be able to find the information you need on your city's Web site.

You must have an EIN before you can apply for your local business permit(s).

In addition, you must be able to show that you already have registered or reserved your business's fictitious name, if applicable. Filing for your fictitious business name is simple and fast and requires a nominal fee. You can apply for a fictitious name statement (or DBA) with the county where your business is located, through the county recorder's office.

Home Occupation Permit

If you have opted to work from a home office, chances are you will need to secure a home occupation permit. You will either have to pay an annual fee or a percentage of your annual profits to keep your home occupation permit current. Someone at your local city hall will be able to tell you if you need a home occupation permit and what you need to do to apply for one.

Zoning Permit

Again, if you are working from a home office, you may be required to apply for a zoning permit. Talk with someone at your local city hall to determine if you need to secure a zoning permit to work from your home.

In addition, if you live in a condominium or live in a community run by a homeowners' association, you will likely need to get permission to operate your business from home. Unfortunately, there are some homeowners' associations and landlords who do not allow people to run businesses from their homes. In some cases, if you have a homeowners' association or a landlord, you may be severely restricted in the type of home-based business you run and how you run it.

Resale Permit, If Selling a Product

If you will be selling products from your home, you may need to secure a resale permit. Some states require resale permits while others do not, so be sure to contact your Secretary of State to determine your state's particular requirements. While many states require resale permits, you will find that the actual name for the permit varies. A resale permit also may be called a resale certificate, a certificate of authority, a resale license, a seller's permit, a resale number, a permit sales and use tax, a transaction privilege sales tax, or an application to collect/report tax.

Often issued by a state's franchise board or department of revenue, a resale permit allows business owners to purchase items at wholesale prices without having to pay sales tax. You will not pay tax on the items you will be using for resale, provided you actually sell those products to consumers. If you intend to use the products solely for yourself, you will not receive the tax reprieve.

If your business structure is a corporation, you may not need a resale permit. If your business is a corporation, you can use your federal tax identification when you purchase wholesale products that you plan to resell.

To determine if you need to apply for a resale permit and for information on how to apply for that permit, contact the city hall or Chamber of Commerce in your city or town.

Sales Tax, If Selling a Product

If you will be selling a product or service that is subject to sales tax, you will need to pass that cost on to your customers. After your customers pay the sales tax, you will take that sales tax and pay it to the appropriate state, county, and city agencies. Because you will have a resale permit, you will not have to pay sales tax; only your customers will have to pay it.

Note that Alaska, Delaware, New Hampshire, Montana, and Oregon do not charge sales tax. Additionally, be fully aware that some counties, towns, and cities charge their own sales taxes in addition to those imposed by the state.

Employer Identification Number

An employer identification number is a requirement for all business entities, except sole proprietorships. Even if you do not currently have or plan to have employees, according to the law, you must still obtain an EIN. Issued by the IRS, EINs distinguish business entities.

Fortunately, applying for an EIN is simple, quick, and free. There are several ways of applying for an EIN, including:

- **Phone.** You can call the IRS's toll-free number, 1-800-829-4933, between 7 a.m. and 3 p.m. local time Monday through Friday. You will be required to answer several questions, after which you will be assigned an EIN. If you are applying by phone, it is a good idea to go to the IRS Web site to print out the form. Then fill it out as completely as possible so you have the answers to the questions you will be asked during the phone conversation.

- **Fax.** To apply for an EIN number by fax, you need to complete IRS Form SS-4, which you can find online at **sa2.www4.irs.gov/ sa_vign/newFormSS4.do**. After the IRS reviews your application, it will determine if your business is required to have an EIN. If it is determined you need an EIN, you will receive your number within four business days. Remember to provide the IRS with a fax number to which it can send the EIN.

To fax Form SS-4 to the IRS, go to the particular IRS page that lists the fax numbers for each of the 50 states. You can find all the fax numbers online at **www.irs.gov/file/article/0,,id=111453,00.html**.

- **Online.** To apply online, fill out Form SS-4: **sa2.www4.irs.gov/ sa_vign/newFormSS4.do**. When you hit the submit button, you will either receive your EIN or be told that you have left out important information. When the application is completed correctly, you will be given your EIN.

- **Mail.** Again, you will have to complete Form SS-4 (sa2.**www4 .irs.gov/sa_vign/newFormSS4.do**) and then mail the completed application to the IRS. For those applying for an EIN by mail, the wait is generally four weeks until a number is issued.

Should your business change ownership, or if you change the structure of your business (if you go from an LLC to a corporation, for example), you must apply for a new EIN. You can determine whether you need to file for a new EIN by visiting the IRS requirement page at **www.irs.gov/ businesses/small/article/0,,id=98011,00.html**.

To replace a lost or misplaced EIN, call 1-800-829-4933 between 7 a.m. and 3 p.m. local time, Monday through Friday. Keep your EIN in several places so it is easy to find to avoid having to go through the hassle of reapplying.

chapter 6

All About Insurance for Your Business and for Yourself

Owning a small business can be a hazardous experience. Many unexpected events happen that can put your business and your own personal funds in jeopardy. Finding good business insurance for these many occurrences should be one of the first things you do when setting up your business. This section will provide a review of the types of insurance you need to consider purchasing and some of the features you should look for.

Tips for Finding Health Insurance

With the cost of health insurance rising at astronomical rates, one of the scariest things about being self-employed is going without health insurance. For most small-business people, purchasing health insurance is too costly to be considered. Be aware that there are alternatives that might help keep these costs down. You can get quotes for health insurance for yourself and your employees from online resources (such as **www.ehealthinsurance .com**) or through a local insurance broker.

Here are some points you will need to consider before you purchase health insurance:

1. **Provider networks/PPO plans.** A PPO (Preferred Provider Organization) selects doctors, hospitals, and other providers to join

their plan. Do you have a specific doctor or hospital or specialists that you want to use? If so, you should check to see if they are part of the provider network of any health plan you join. You may still be able to use the services of these providers, even if they are not in the network, but you will be paying higher out-of-network fees for their services.

2. **Deductible.** The higher the deductible you can afford, the lower the monthly cost of your insurance. If you can pay a higher deductible, you can save on insurance costs.

3. **Co-insurance.** Co-insurance is the amount of each claim you pay, in conjunction with the insurance company. For example, for a plan with a 20 percent co-pay, you pay 20 percent of the cost of an office visit, and the insurance company pays the other 80 percent. You may be able to save on monthly premiums if you agree to accept a higher co-pay amount.

4. **Basic versus extended coverage.** Depending on the amount of money you can afford to pay out-of-pocket, you might consider buying the minimum basic (sometimes called "major medical") coverage. This coverage would pay only for catastrophic illnesses or injuries, leaving you to pay for routine and preventative care. Major medical insurance is much less expensive than basic coverage.

5. **Preventative services.** Consider a plan that has preventative services, including annual physical exams or tests (such as mammograms). Although this type of plan is typically more expensive, it might save you money in the long run by finding problems early.

6. **Prescription drugs.** Since prescription drug costs continue to rise and most people need or will need maintenance drugs, look for a plan with prescription drug insurance. Also look carefully at what

drugs the plan pays for, particularly if you are on maintenance drugs. Some plans limit drug payments to generic drugs, and some have extremely limited formularies (lists of drugs included in the plan). Of course, the better the drug coverage, the more expensive the plan, so weigh your need for continuing drugs or other health supplies with your wish to keep premium costs down.

7. **Dental coverage.** Some insurance plans provide dental coverage, but many offer it as a separate plan. Depending on the level of coverage you want, and whether you want orthodontia (braces) covered, you may want to add this coverage.

8. **Maternity coverage.** If you are creating a plan for yourself and you do not plan on having children (or more children), you can save money by not including maternity coverage in your plan. On the other hand, your employees may want this benefit.

9. **Claims service.** When you have narrowed down your choice of carriers, ask each to provide you with information about current policyholders. Then call these companies and ask about claims service. The cheapest insurance is not a good buy if you find out that the claims service is poor.

A new alternative type of health insurance is called a Health Savings Account (HSA), which allows you to put aside a certain amount of pre-tax money (up to $1,500 each year) into a special bank account to be used only for specified health care expenses. The amount set aside in the savings plan is used to pay the deductible and co-pay amounts, leaving the insurance company to pay only for costs over the deductible and for higher-cost and more catastrophic incidents.

HSA plans have several benefits. First, they reduce the cost of your health insurance, since the insurance company is expected to pay less and only for higher-cost, less likely expenses. Second, your deductions into the HSA are pre-tax, so you save money on your taxes each year. Third, you can accumulate the amount in the HSA account; you do not have to use the whole amount each year. In this way, you may have more money available to use as you get older and have more health care expenses or after retirement to use for health expenses.

You can set up an HSA account at many financial institutions. Most of these accounts are interest-bearing and have monthly or quarterly maintenance fees. They often provide a debit card you can use for paying for health care services. As more people become familiar with HSA accounts, they will be used more to save on health insurance costs, benefiting both insurance companies and health care customers.

Finding Disability Insurance

A small-business owner who is relying on income from the business to provide for a family and cover living expenses should consider buying disability insurance immediately after opening the business.

The price for disability insurance is based on a number of factors, including these:

- **Elimination period length** – The period of time at the beginning of the policy during which disability is not covered; this may be as long as two years

- **Benefit period** – The maximum time during which benefits may be paid

- **Age of insured**

- **Occupation of insured,** based on the risk of injury or accident in each occupation and the cost of replacing income for different occupations

- **Benefit amount** – The amount of monthly benefits paid for various levels of disability

Disability benefits may be paid for total disability, which is the inability to perform the major aspects of your position. Disability insurance also typically includes recovery benefits, which are paid during the time you are recovering. Some disability insurance companies also offer business overhead insurance, which provides for coverage for overhead expenses of the business during the time you are disabled. For quotes on disability insurance, you can check online or through a local business insurance company.

The Importance of Business Property Insurance

What would you do if your computer was destroyed in a fire? This is just one of many possible disasters that could strike your small business and that should be insured against. If you are seeking funding for your new business from a bank or another lender, the lender most likely will require you to have business property/casualty/liability insurance. Even if you do not need funding, you need to get business insurance coverage soon after opening.

A basic business insurance policy includes three sections:

1. **Property/casualty insurance.** This coverage pays for damage to your business property in the event it is destroyed due to natural disaster (e.g., a hurricane or tornado), a fire, or some other event. If you own the building or home where your business is located, that structure should be insured. If you are renting office space, that structure is covered through the landlord's policy; some landlords

also require you to have coverage on your property within the office. Your business equipment and other property are also included in your business insurance coverage. When considering costs for this coverage, weigh carefully the cost of replacement coverage; while it is more expensive to pay for replacement value, the cost of buying new equipment and furniture keeps going up, and used furniture has almost no value. If your computer were destroyed, for example, and you did not have replacement coverage, the amount the insurance company would give you for your old computer would not even begin to be enough to pay for a new computer.

2. **Business interruption insurance.** In the event that your business or office was destroyed, this insurance would cover your ongoing expenses during the time you could not operate your business. Coverage is based on your estimated sales and expenses during this time, which is a good reason for saving copies of your income statement and balance sheet outside your office, so you can substantiate these amounts.

3. **Liability insurance.** The liability portion of your coverage provides you with protection in the event that you are sued by someone for negligence. For example, if you have an office location and a customer is injured while in your office, he or she can sue you for negligence. Your liability insurance is the most expensive part of your business insurance, because the settlement amounts can be very high.

For more information on specific provisions of business insurance coverage, do not hesitate to get quotes from several companies. It is often a good idea to purchase your business insurance from the same company where you have your personal insurance coverage, because you can get an "umbrella" liability policy that provides extra coverage in the event you are sued.

Car Insurance

If you use your car for business purposes or if you have purchased a car or truck for your business, you will need business auto coverage. The cost of this insurance will depend on the mileage, how many people will be driving and their ages and driving records, and the value of the vehicle. Check around for costs of coverage, making your primary consideration the claims service provided by each company. An insurance company that can pay your claim and help you get your vehicle repaired quickly can save you dollars in lost sales and lower expenses.

Workers' Compensation Insurance

If you have employees, you will need to purchase workers' compensation insurance; this coverage is not included in the typical business owner's insurance policy described above. Workers' compensation provisions and costs vary by state; most states require coverage to be maintained by business owners who employ more than one or two people. Check online (or in the Resource section at the end of this book) for links to information about workers' compensation laws in your state.

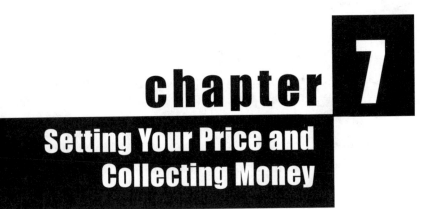

chapter 7

Setting Your Price and Collecting Money

As an entrepreneur and self-employed professional, you have the right to set your own prices for your services and/or products. When you have determined how much you will charge your customers, you will have to begin promoting your business and your services/products.

Fortunately, marketing your new business is not difficult, and even if you are on a shoestring budget, you can spread the word about your services/products for relatively little.

Tips for Setting Your Prices

Services

If you are providing professional services to clients, there are several ways you can set your fees:

- **Hourly.** Some professionals, like attorneys and accountants, bill at an hourly rate. They keep track of all work done for a client and provide a bill when the work is completed. You should set your hourly rate to be competitive with other similar professionals in your field. Check with a professional association in your field to see what rates are in your region.

- **Flat fee.** For some types of work and in some professional fields, a flat fee is the usual charge. A CPA, for example, might have a flat fee for doing a typical tax return for a sole proprietorship. Freelance writers usually accept flat fees for contract work, as do some engineers, based on the estimated time for the job.

- **Retainer.** Other professionals, such as virtual assistants (VAs), have a monthly minimum that is charged to their clients, based on an hourly rate and a minimum number of hours. The client must pay the minimum rate, no matter how few hours the VA works. If the VA works more than the minimum, the hourly rate is charged for additional time.

As you can see, setting fees is dependent on the type of work you do. It is also to a large degree dependent on the fees set by your competitors, because you do not want to be too high or too low in comparison. If your fees are too high, you may not get as much work as you would like. The more common problem among professionals is setting fees too low. In the minds of many clients, low fees are a sign that you do not value your work very highly. Set your fees in the middle to high side of the range of your competitors.

To determine these rates, spend time online searching for fees in your profession, or find others in your profession and ask what they charge. It is not uncommon for professionals to be willing to share their fee structures, and many times a little searching will provide you with the range of fees.

Before you begin to offer your services, prepare a client agreement form and decide on your terms of service. Here are some questions you will need to answer about your fee structure:

1. If you are going to charge an hourly rate, will there be a minimum amount for each assignment?

2. If you decide on flat fees for certain assignments or projects, what will those fees be? In other words, how much is reasonable for each type of project?

3. If you want to work on retainer, what is the minimum monthly amount you will accept? For hourly work beyond the retainer amount, what will you charge?

4. When do you expect payment on flat fee assignments? Do you want an amount at the beginning, middle, and end? Or will you wait until the end for payment? Do these payment terms depend on the total of the project?

Accepting Payments

How will you accept payment? By check? By credit card? By PayPal? Before you begin your first professional project, you will need to set up the means by which you can be paid. One of the easiest ways to accept payment is by establishing a PayPal account. PayPal takes payments from clients and transfers them to your bank account. Usually it only takes a day or two to process U.S. payments using this service. Payments to and from other countries will take a longer amount of time.

For credit card payments, you will need to set up a merchant account. This is an account with a bank that processes payments for you. This process is explained in more detail later in this chapter.

Products

If your product is available from other vendors, find out what they are charging for this product. Prices sometimes vary by region, but for the most part in our online economy they tend to be fairly close throughout the country.

Refunds

You will need to prepare and display a refund policy for your products or services. The manner in which you accept refunds can be a benefit to you as a customer service. Gladly accepting refunds on products or services, particularly if you are offering something new that people are not sure about, is an excellent way to get people to try something without concern about being stuck with something they do not want or need. If you give refunds cheerfully and quickly with no questions asked, people feel that you stand behind your product or service.

Consider offering a full refund on products if returned in original condition or unused within 30 days. For products purchased on the Internet, you usually can state that you will refund the purchase price minus return shipping.

For services, you might want to offer a guarantee that the person may cancel at any time within 30 days if not satisfied. Of course, you take the risk that the person will use your service or download your product and then ask for a refund.

Getting Paid

One of the biggest concerns of the self-employed professional is getting paid in a timely manner. When it comes to getting paid, working for yourself is far different than working for someone else. As an employee, you know you are going to be paid every week, every other week, or once a month. You always know a paycheck is forthcoming. When you work for yourself, on the other hand, your payments may be sporadic. Even if you tell clients that payment is due upon completion of your work, you still may have to wait.

Unfortunately, the majority of self-employed professionals have dealt with clients who simply refuse to pay, who stop answering phone calls, or who disappear when a completed project is in their hands. Those clients who refuse to pay often do so because they know that some self-employed professionals will not have the funds or the inclination to fight for the money they earned.

But do not let that fact get you down when it comes to working for yourself. There are several ways you can protect yourself to ensure that you get paid.

Have a written agreement. Always have a written agreement with the client. Never rely solely on an oral agreement, because they can be difficult to prove if you take the client to court. When you do not have a written agreement, your client can say that you did not provide the work as you promised (even if you have) or that you agreed to a lower price.

We will discuss in depth how you can create a client agreement, including all the terms and provisions that should be a part of all client contracts, in Chapter 11.

Get a deposit. Always ask for a 50 percent deposit from your clients, especially new clients and those clients with money troubles. That way, if the client disappears after you have turned over the completed project, you have at least been paid half of the fee. You do not always have to get a deposit from clients with whom you have established solid business relationships, but keep in mind that getting a deposit is security if the client should disappear.

Another advantage of asking for a deposit or a down payment is the fact that it illustrates to clients that you are serious about your business and you are serious about getting paid. A client who pays a deposit is also showing you that he is serious about paying you.

Check for a purchase order. Ask the client if he or she requires a purchase order. In some instances, a client will want you to obtain and submit a signed purchase order regardless of whether you already have signed a contract. Ask clients about a purchase order before you begin a project to save you payment headaches later on.

Create a payment schedule. If you are working with a client on a long-term project, one that is going to last three months or more, have a payment schedule in place so you do not have to wait for payment until the project is completed. An ideal way to work with a payment schedule is to require the client to pay one-third upon starting the project, one-third when you are halfway through with the project, and one-third when you finish the project.

Being paid periodically is a good way to protect yourself. Should your client fail to make his second payment, for example, you can inform him that you are stopping work until you receive payment. In some instances, that will prompt clients to pay. But, in other cases, it makes no difference. The good news: At least you got paid for some of the work you did, and you know not to work with that client again.

Ask for a personal guarantee. Asking for a personal guarantee is similar to asking someone to cosign for you on a loan. For example, if you will be working with someone who is a member of an LLC, you can ask the owners of that LLC to provide you with a written personal guarantee. That way, if the person whom you are working with defaults on the payment, the owners of the LLC will make that payment. A personal guarantee is a legally binding document, and you can sue if the LLC owners refuse to pay you.

You can either have the personal guarantee included in your written agreement with the LLC or create a separate document stating that the named owners promise to make payment if the person you are working with fails to pay.

Set project milestones. Along the lines of using a payment schedule, if you are going to be working on a big project, consider setting project milestones. Let us say you are writing a book, which requires extensive research and interviewing, for a company. Consider breaking that project into milestones. For example, set a date for the completion of the research phase. On that date you show the company the research you have compiled, and you receive payment. Your next milestone might be the writing of the first three chapters. You turn them in on the set date and then are paid. Milestones are a good way to keep track of long projects and to ensure prompt payment. Again, if a client fails to make one of the scheduled payments, simply stop working until he or she does pay.

Run a credit check. Do a credit check on your potential clients. It may sound excessive, but it is not. A credit check will help you determine whether a client or a company has a history of prompt payments or if there have been several missed payments.

Of course, you do not have to do a credit check on a well-known, established company; but you should at least invest the time in doing a credit check on those businesses or clients of whom you have never heard.

You can obtain a prospective client's credit in one of two ways. You can ask the client to provide you with his or her credit information and credit references. If a client refuses to give you credit information, reconsider doing business with him or her. Additionally, be aware that, by asking for credit references, you may not discover whether the client is actually a good credit risk, as he may simply refer you to people with whom he has not yet had a problem.

Another way you can check a prospective client's credit is to request a credit check from a credit agency, such as Experian (**www.experian.com**), Equifax (**www.equifax.com**), TransUnion (**www.transunion.com**), or Dun & Bradstreet (**www.dnb.com**).

Although doing a business credit check this way is more time consuming and will include a fee, you should take the time to do the credit check now rather than risk working with someone who may not pay you.

Creating an Online Payment Processing System

Before you begin selling products or services in person or online, you will need to set up a merchant account to make it easier for customers to pay you with a credit card or debit card. Even if you are selling at a booth outdoors or at an expo, if you have access to the Internet, you can process credit and debit cards online. Here is how this process works:

1. You as the merchant swipe the credit or debit card through your processor, or you input the transaction information online. The processor connects with the Internet through a payment gateway.

2. The gateway passes the transaction to your bank processor.

3. The bank processor submits it to a credit card exchange. The exchange is a network of financial entities that communicate with each other.

4. The exchange routes the transaction information to the buyer's card issuer, which checks to see if the merchant information is correct, if the card is active, and if the buyer has available credit.

5. The buyer's card issuer approves or denies the transaction and passes the result (approval or denial) back to the exchange.

6. The exchange relays the information back to your bank processor, which in turn relays it back to the gateway.

7. The gateway informs you that the buyer's credit is good or bad, stores the information, and produces a receipt.

This process is conducted within three seconds or less.

Because so many people assume that merchants will be able to process their credit card or debit card transaction, it has become a requirement for businesses that sell products or services to set up this service. At the most basic level, you will need:

- **An account with a payment gateway provider.** Commonly called a "gateway," this provider is the intermediary between the buyer's account, the bank, and your account. For online sales, the gateway sets up a page to capture the information from the buyer, including name, address, and credit card information. The gateway then verifies the credit card information and transmits the charge from the buyer's account to yours. For in-person sales, the gateway transmits the credit card information that is swiped, along with a pin or an acceptance code, to the bank.

- **A merchant account with a bank.** Your merchant account at the bank sends the verified transaction to your checking account.

- **An Internet account.** You will need an account with an Internet service provider where you can set up your gateway.

If you are selling online, you will also need:

- **A Web site.** Your Web site is used as an online shop where you display your merchandise or describe your services, so people will know what they are buying. You also will need to explain your refund and privacy policies on your Web site.

- **A "shopping cart."** There are a number of online services that provide shopping cart software capabilities. If you are selling products online, for example, your customers need to be able to select products and choose number, color, and style and to collect this merchandise in the shopping cart. They also need to be able to take items out of the shopping cart and to see the final total. When the customer is ready to purchase, he or she is taken to the gateway page where the information for purchase, including credit card information, is input.

If you have only a few items or services to sell, you may be able to use your gateway as a shopping cart. If a customer is reluctant to input credit card information on the Internet, your gateway account will allow you to take the order over the phone and to input it directly into the gateway by viewing an online order page.

If you are selling in person, you will need:

- **A POS terminal.** If you will be processing credit and debit cards in person, you will need to purchase a credit card processing machine, called a point of sale (POS) terminal. If you will be processing debit cards, you probably will need a machine that has a keypad so people can put in their pin numbers.

- **A separate data (phone) line at your business** or wherever your sales take place so you can process transactions without having to tie up your office phone line

Charges for Card Processing

POS terminal cost. You can expect to pay from as little as $100 to over $800 for a machine, depending on whether or not you will accept a used machine. You can get a machine that lets the customer input a pin number for debit cards or one that produces a paper receipt to be signed by the customer. The paper in these cases is two-part NCR paper so the customer copy can be used as a receipt. You also may be able to find a used terminal through eBay or your bank.

Setup costs charged by the gateway and merchant bank (some of these costs may be waived as promotion by either vendor):

- Application fee

- Gateway setup fee

- Merchant bank setup fee

- Programming fee (probably not applicable)

- Setup fees for specific credit cards (Discover and American Express)

Monthly processing fees:

- Per transaction discount fee (not a discount to you, but a fee you pay to the gateway); typically set from 1.5 to 2.5 percent, depending on the volume of transactions you have each month. The higher the volume of transactions, the lower the fee for each transaction.

- A transaction fee (to the merchant bank), around 25 cents per transaction.

- A monthly minimum/monthly statement fee. Some merchants have a monthly minimum of about $25, which you must pay even if you process no transactions in a month.

- A monthly maintenance fee, usually for sellers who sell products on the Internet.

- Monthly minimums or specific fees for certain credit cards.

Application fees are commonly waived as a marketing device, so you probably will not have to pay that. Here is a summary of the common fees you can expect to pay each month:

- Monthly customer service fee: $25

- Monthly minimum for MasterCard/Visa: $15

- Monthly gateway fee: $19.99

- Monthly paper statement fee: $7.95

- Qualified discount rate: 1.5 to 2.5 cents per transaction

You will be asked to sign a contract with the gateway for a minimum number of months (six months or more), and if you cancel within that time you will have to pay penalties. Compare charges carefully before signing with a payment gateway. What looks like a great deal because of a low discount rate may be worse than another processor that charges a higher discount rate and no add-on fees.

Here are some questions to ask yourself before you set up your merchant account:

1. **What kind of transactions will you be processing?** For most retail and service businesses, you will be processing credit cards face-to-face, with the customer handing you a card and you swiping it, inputting the amount, having the customer sign, and waiting for the credit card transaction to be approved. If you plan to sell products, this process works the same way.

2. **How many transactions will you be processing each month?** Of course, this amount will grow as you gain new customers, so look toward the largest number you think you will be processing each month.

3. **What gateway and merchant will you use?** If you already have a banking relationship with one bank, talk with that bank first.

Using the same bank for all your transactions will make processing and recording transactions much easier. Your bank also likely will have a gateway it prefers to use. However, before you sign up with your bank, check costs. Some banks charge extremely high fees, and it might make more sense for you to go elsewhere for these services. Note also that you do not have to go to a bank; you can use an online service instead.

4. **What kind of card processing unit (POS terminal) will you need?** For in-person transactions, find a terminal that is relatively inexpensive and that will produce a paper receipt and copy. If you are processing debit transactions, you will need a keypad so people can input their pin numbers.

5. **Will you need an additional phone line?** If you are going to process in-person transactions, you will need a separate dedicated phone line. Although this may seem like an unnecessary expense, consider that having one phone line for both phone calls and Internet transactions means that a phone call in one part of your office might interrupt a transaction or that you might need to keep customers waiting to process a credit card transaction until the phone line is not tied up. Most businesses quickly find that they need that second line. It might be more expensive to have two lines, but they will save you time and improve customer service.

6. **What cards will you take?** You probably will need to accept the most common credit cards, but you also may have customers who want to use others. Here is a partial list:

   - VISA

   - MasterCard

   - American Express

- Diner's Club

- Discover

Except for MasterCard and VISA, these card companies charge a separate fee to process transactions and some require a monthly minimum, no matter how many transactions you process. You might want to begin processing only these two cards and then add others if you have many customers who want to use them.

After you have made your decisions, based on the issues above, and you have purchased the required equipment and services, you probably will need someone to help you set up the system. If you are selling online, your Web person should be able to help. If you are selling in person, you can often ask for someone from the bank to set up the equipment and walk you through the process.

Deduct Bad Debts From Your Income Taxes

Of course, no matter how much you protect yourself, you are going to deal with clients who simply do not pay, no matter how hard you pursue them. Unfortunately, you will likely not be able to deduct a bad debt from your income taxes, because you, as a self-employed professional, do not report your income until you actually have been paid. Therefore, according to the Internal Revenue Service, you have not lost anything.

As unfair as it may seem, there is no way around this rule. You can, however, take legal action to try to recover the money you are owed.

Invoice Tips

Invoicing is a simple but effective way to bill your clients and to keep track of the work you have done and the money you have earned. Creating an invoice is very simple. The basic information that every invoice should contain includes:

- The name of the person to whom the invoice is addressed

- Your name and contact information, including address, phone number, fax, and e-mail

- An invoice number

- The date

- A purchase order, if applicable

- A contract number, if applicable

- The dates of the services performed; for example, June 2 through June 12, 2007

- A description of the services provided

- A list of expenses, if applicable

- The total amount due

- The date payment is due (e.g., "Net 10" means the invoice is due ten days from the date of the invoice)

- A discount percentage, if applicable. Some businesses and self-employed professionals offer a discount for those clients who pay the invoice in full by the due date.

- Percentage of a late fee. If a client fails to pay by the due date, you may want to institute a late fee.

Always send your invoice as soon after the work has been completed as possible. Failing to send an invoice immediately, instead of waiting a week or two, could cause your payment to be delayed. By that time, your client very well may have forgotten about the project or it may no longer be one of his priorities.

You also must ask the client how he prefers to be invoiced: Will he accept a faxed or e-mail invoice, or does he prefer a hard copy of the invoice? Always keep a copy of the invoice you have sent with the date.

Determining Your Terms of Payment

You perform work, and you must be paid for that work. The question you must consider is, How long do you wait for payment after you have given a client a completed project? Setting your terms of payment is extremely important.

Always discuss your payment terms with a prospective client before you begin working. Standard terms of business are usually 30, 60, or 90 days. Like most self-employed professionals, you probably want to be paid as soon as a project is completed. Or you may opt to give your clients seven or 15 days to pay. The decision is yours, but make sure the payment terms are clearly stated in your written agreement or contract.

Dealing With Delinquent Clients

You must have a plan of action for dealing with delinquent clients. If late fees are not enough of an incentive for your client to pay, you will need to be proactive in collecting your money.

First, you must have some sort of accounting system in place, so you know which invoices have been sent, which have been paid, and which are overdue. When you know an invoice is overdue, you then can take action.

Start by contacting the client when the due date rolls around and you have still not been paid. SCORE recommends first faxing the client with a reminder that the invoice is currently due. A fax, according to SCORE, is often seen as a sign of urgency. If, after sending the invoice via fax, you do not receive a response, call the client as a gentle reminder.

You may find that faxing and calling just does not work. That is when you will want to become firm. You can be firm without being rude. Send a collection letter to the client, stating that the account is overdue and how much is owed. Keep a copy of the collection letter for your own records.

Throughout your collection efforts, no matter how frustrated and angry you become, always remain professional. Never threaten, harass, or use derogatory language with the client.

Next, you should send an invoice with the words "Second Notice" on top. After you send the second notice, continue to send an invoice on a monthly basis, with the late fee (if you have one) added to the total amount. Again, do not threaten the client.

Dealing With a Client Who Refuses to Pay

Sometimes, no matter how proactive you are, a client simply is going to refuse to pay. In such cases, you have several legal options to help you collect the money you are owed. Before you take legal action, you must send a final letter to the client informing him of the action you will take if he fails to pay. That action may be turning him over to a collection agency or suing him for the full amount owed. Give the client a firm date by which he must pay before you take legal action.

Sometimes a final demand letter will do the trick, but do not count on it. Once the final deadline you have given the client passes, you can take action in one of several ways: hire a collection agency, sue the client in small-claims court, hire an attorney, sue the client in a state court, or go to arbitration.

Remember that, when you take legal action, the client who is not paying may never want to work with you again. Be absolutely sure that is a risk you are willing to take. There are times when legitimate businesspeople fail to pay because they simply do not have the money at the time and are too embarrassed to say anything. If your client always has paid promptly in the past, perhaps there is a reason for his failure to pay this time.

Collection agency. If you have ever failed to pay a bill for a period of time, you likely have been contacted by a collection agency. A collection agency is hired on behalf of the person or company that is owed money to try to collect that money.

Rather than charging a fee for using its services, a collection agency generally just takes a cut of the payment that is made. Payment runs from 15 to 50 percent of the debt, depending on several factors, such as the age of the debt.

A collection agency will work on your behalf to collect full payment of the debt owed. The biggest challenge you likely will have is finding a collection agency willing to work with you, since you are self-employed with a small business. Still, ask other professionals if they know of a good collection agency who works with the self-employed.

When you find a collection agency to work with, make sure you get the agreement in writing, including the fee the collection agency is going to take.

Small-claims court. If your claim is less than a certain amount of money (between $5,000 and $7,500, depending on the state), you can take your client to small-claims court. The best part of small-claims court is the fact that you do not need an attorney, and the majority of cases heard in the court deal with debt collection.

If the client owes you more than is allowed in small-claims court, you can either pursue the claim (losing that money that goes over the limit) or take other legal action.

Hire an attorney. The first thing an attorney can do for you is write a letter to the client who is not paying his bill. An attorney's letter can be much more effective than a letter from you. In some cases, an attorney's letter will scare the client into paying.

If you decide to hire an attorney to sue for the money that is owed to you, be sure of two things. First, make sure the debt is worth the money it is going to cost you. Second, be sure the client has the money to pay.

State court. Going to state court – also known as superior or municipal court – is another option. Many times, however, the case never gets to the courtroom, and the defendant settles out of court. You do not need a lawyer to take your case to a state court, but you may want to have one on retainer should you have questions or need help in preparing your legal strategy.

Arbitration. Does your written agreement include a clause for arbitration? You may want to consider having an arbitration clause written into your contract if you do not have one already. However, be aware that, if you have an arbitration clause, you cannot sue the client in any court, small claims or otherwise.

Like small-claims court, arbitration is inexpensive and quick. Unlike small-claims court, where a judge presides over the proceedings, arbitration is overseen by an arbitrator. The arbitrator will decide either in your favor or in the client's favor. Should the arbitrator rule in your favor, the ruling will be enforced just as it would be in court.

chapter 8

Ways to Market Your Product or Service

Network

One of the best ways to spread the word about your business is to network with people in your community and online. Networking allows you to build your credibility within the community and your particular industry, and it helps you cultivate business relationships with other self-employed, small-business owners.

Successful business relationships always should be a two-way street: You benefit in some form from the relationship, as does the other person. For example, you are at a conference or even a Chamber of Commerce event, and you meet a writer. You are a Web designer in search of a way to increase your client base. The writer you meet is doing the same. You chat for a while and realize that together you can combine your services to attract new clients. You exchange numbers and e-mail addresses and make plans to discuss your ideas further. That is a prime example of networking. When done right, networking is extremely effective.

The best thing about networking is you can do it virtually anywhere. Just start talking to people; you never know whom you might meet. Some of the many ways you can network both online and offline are:

- Attend Chamber of Commerce events.

- Carry business cards with you everywhere you go. (Remember the two-card rule. Always give the person two business cards: one for him- or herself and one to pass along.)

- Go online and find message boards related to your craft (i.e., graphic design) and start talking to other people in the field.

- Join industry organizations.

- Read the local newspaper for articles about people or other businesses in your industry, and then contact those people.

- Start a blog and update it often.

- Ask for and give referrals. When you are given a referral, call that person as soon as possible.

- Always follow up with contacts.

- Volunteer in your community.

- Attend conferences and trade shows.

- Host a lunch or dinner and invite local businesspeople to attend.

- Join clubs and organizations in your industry.

If you are creative, you likely can find dozens of different ways to network with other businesspeople. But make sure you also network socially. You may go to a function at your child's school, for example, and chat with other parents. Through chatting you may find new business contacts. Remember to constantly be on the lookout for networking opportunities.

Networking Tips

Networking requires effort on your part. There is far more to networking than chatting with others and handing out a few business cards. To successfully network, you must work at it. To ensure your success at networking, try the following:

- **Always be positive.** When you are positive, there is a much higher likelihood that others are going to respond to you favorably.

- **Be yourself.** Do not pretend you are something you are not.

- **Do not just do the talking** – Be an active listener and show the person who is talking that you are really interested in what they are saying.

- **Network everywhere you go.** From industry conferences to waiting in line at the bank, you never know whom you may meet.

- **Treat your customers well.** When customers are treated well, they will be much more inclined to refer your business to friends and loved ones.

- **Stay in touch with contacts you have made**, even if it is just by sending a polite e-mail.

- **Always follow up when you are given a referral**, and do not forget to thank the person who gave you that referral.

Establish a Web Presence

As we previously discussed, a Web site is no longer a luxury for businesses. It quickly has become a necessity. If you want your business to become and stay competitive, you must have a Web site. A Web site is your online business card, and if you are selling your services or products, it also can act as your virtual storefront.

If you are just making the transition from employee to self-employed professional, you may be tight on funds. The good news is, if you cannot afford a professional Web designer now, you still can have an attractive, functional, professional-looking Web site.

You have two main options for creating a Web site if you are short on funds. First, you may want to consider contacting your local community colleges and universities to see if there is a student interested in designing your Web site for a nominal fee, a testimonial, and the opportunity to use the Web site in his or her portfolio.

If you would rather design the Web site yourself and you have little experience, all you need is a Web template and a Web design program like FrontPage or Dreamweaver. You can find thousands of Web templates online that either are free or cost under $100.

With a Web template, you can customize it to your needs, and then add your own content in the template and publish to the Web.

Of course, with a Web site, you also will need a domain name and Web hosting. You generally can purchase Web hosting for less than $10 a month. Make sure you never purchase your Web hosting and your domain name from the same company. Additionally, when you register a domain name, make sure that you, not the hosting company, own the domain name. If you purchase a domain name and the company owns the domain name, it can charge you as much as its wants for the registration fee every year. On top of that, you will have a difficult, if not impossible, time taking the domain name to a new company.

When your Web site is online, start promoting it by submitting it to search engines, adding it to your business card, and writing a press release introducing your business.

Create a Logo

What are some of the logos with which you are familiar? The golden arches of McDonald's? The swoosh of Nike? Pillsbury's doughboy?

A good logo creates brand recognition. You may not need a logo; however, a logo can help you brand your business, product, or service.

Even if you are on a tight budget, consider creating a logo now rather than later. In addition to helping create brand recognition, a logo will do several things:

- You will stand out among the competition, especially those who do not have a logo.

- A logo will make your small business appear larger than it is.

- Your business will appear as though it is established.

Join Your Local Chamber of Commerce

Joining your local Chamber of Commerce can be an ideal way to get to know other business owners in your community. Local chapters of the Chamber of Commerce generally hold business events at least once a month, during which business owners in the area gather to socialize and network. You never know whom you might meet at one of these events, so consider attending as many events as you can.

Individual Chamber of Commerce organizations often offer their members numerous perks, including discounted health insurance plans, special advertising deals, and a listing in the Chamber of Commerce directory.

There is also a National Chamber of Commerce, which can be found online at **www.uschamber.com/default** and offers members valuable networking and educational opportunities, and other programs designed to help entrepreneurs and small-business owners.

Join the Better Business Bureau

The Better Business Bureau will help lend credibility to your business and will help your customers feel secure in doing business with you. Unhappy customers take their complaints to the Better Business Bureau, which, in turn, contacts the business named in the complaint to give that business a chance to either respond or rectify the problem.

When a prospective customer or client goes to the Better Business Bureau to check you out, he or she will be able to determine if there have ever been any complaints against you.

There is both an offline BBB and an online BBB. To become a member of the online Better Business Bureau, you must be a member of your local, offline Better Business Bureau. To join, you must meet strict criteria, including but not limited to the following:

- You must have been in business in your area for at least six months.

- You must pay annual dues.

- You must follow all BBB policies.

- You must provide the BBB with all the business information it requests.

- You must answer all complaints promptly.

You can read the exact requirements of joining the Better Business Bureau online at **www.bbb.org/membership/standards.asp**.

If you want to join the online version of the Better Business Bureau, you also must meet certain additional criteria, including:

- Your business must be at least one year old.

- You must be a member of your local Better Business Bureau.

- You must have responded satisfactorily to all complaints.

- You must agree to dispute resolution.

When you are a member of the Better Business Bureau online, you can apply for the Reliability Seal. Learn more online at **www.bbbonline .org**.

Place an Ad in Your Local Yellow Pages

Although everyone does business online today, people still tend to use their local Yellow Pages to look up businesses in their area. Consider placing an ad in your local Yellow Pages to reach prospective customers. In order to add to the value of your Yellow Pages ad, you might want to enhance its appeal to potential customers:

- Add a photo of yourself to make people more aware of who you are.

- Add a map of your location to make it easier for people to find your business.

- Provide a list of special benefits you provide that set you apart from other companies offering the same services.

- Provide information about the conveniences you offer, such as prompt service, longer hours, and acceptance of major credit cards.

Some advertisers believe that size and placement of Yellow Pages ads can increase your rate of calls. In your first years of business, getting a loyal following of customers or a continuing stream of new customers is important, so you may need to spend more money on size and placement of advertising.

Create and Use Business Cards

Every self-employed businessperson should have business cards to give to prospective customers and others. The general rule is to always give out two business cards per person: one for the person and one for the person to pass on.

Fortunately, even if you are on a tight budget, you can create business cards for very little, especially if you use a high-quality printer and paper. You can go to your local office supply store and purchase pre-scored business card paper to run through your own printer. These business cards will not look quite as professional, but they do serve the purpose. You also may choose from one of the many companies online that offer business cards. These companies help you select a design for your cards, and then you can order the printing from their online service. The printed cards are delivered to you.

There are two schools of thought as to the design of business cards: Some people prefer to use only one side of the business card, leaving the opposite side free for the person receiving the business card to make notes. Others prefer to use both sides of the business card. It is a matter of personal preference. One of the best uses for the back side of a business card is for a map to your business location. If you are a local business serving many customers in town, consider adding a simple map to the back of your business card to help people find you easily. Another suggestion for the back of your business card is a coupon for a free introductory offer, which will encourage people to bring the card to your business for the first time. If you decide to use the back of your business card, the possibilities are unlimited, depending on your creativity.

Regardless of the type of business cards you have made, get them made and start using them. Some new business owners walk around town handing out business cards to other local businesses. Others give them out at every opportunity, for example, while standing in the supermarket checkout line or at the bank. Placing a business card in someone's hand gives you the opportunity to reach many more people, because people will share a business card with others.

Write and Release a Press Release

Press releases are designed to announce any type of news. You may want to issue a press release when you open your doors for business, when you have an opening, or for a special community activity that you are sponsoring. The format for a press release is fairly simple:

1. First, give the main facts of the event: date, time, place, kind of event, food, and cost (if any).

2. Then, go into detail about the activities at the event. Describe what will take place when. This section should excite the reader's interest in attending your event. Consider what makes this event different from other similar events in your community.

3. If the event is for a charity or another cause, make sure you emphasize the cause and where the proceeds will go.

4. If the event is to promote your business, provide details on your company – when it was or will be opened, who the owners are, and what kinds of services or products are provided. Include other specifics about your business, including hours and location.

Send the press release to all local television and radio stations with a note asking them to use it as a public service announcement. Do the same for local newspapers, including any local free newspapers. You also might consider sending the press release to your local Chamber of Commerce for publication in its newsletter and to other civic organizations for the same purpose.

Some small-business owners find that their press release is more successful if they place follow-up phone calls to all the places they sent the press release, to check to see if the release was received, to answer questions about the event, and to encourage the person to post the press release.

Place Local Advertisements

Local advertising is available to small businesses at various costs. When you are thinking about where to place your local advertisements, the most important considerations are cost and waste. Waste here means paying for advertising that will never reach the people who are in a position to take advantage of it. For example, if you own a gas station, advertising on the local television station will reach thousands of people, most of whom would not drive all the way across town to use your services.

You do not have to spend a lot of money on television or radio advertising for your local business, because there are many possibilities for advertising. Think creatively about the services you provide or the products you sell. Ask yourself where people who would want these services might be found and advertise in those places. For example, if you are a new healthcare provider who provides services to children, think about where you would find groups of children. You might decide to advertise in high school newspapers. If you are advertising primarily to women, there are local women's magazines in which you might want to place an ad.

Billboards are another local advertising medium often overlooked by new businesses. If your funds are limited, check on the possibility of sharing a board with someone. The newer billboards are electronic and change ads every few minutes. The exposure time is less, but you still can be on a billboard at a good location for less cost.

Sponsor a Local Sports Team

Every town generally has its share of children's sports teams. Consider sponsoring one of those teams. By doing so, you will contribute to a good cause and increase your visibility in the community. Additionally, if you purchase team uniforms or T-shirts with the team name and your business name, your business will get exposure every time team members wear their shirts.

Online Advertising

The possibilities for online advertising are unlimited. If you have a specific group of people to whom you are advertising, one of the best ways to reach that group is through Google AdWords. You can target the group you want to reach, create a short ad, and the ad will be placed on the Web sites or blogs of people who are talking to this group. If you sell quilting supplies, for example, and you want to reach quilters, your Google AdSense ad can be placed on quilting blogs and Web sites for quilters. Each time someone clicks on your ad, you pay a small fee to Google. Advertising directly online to people who might use your products or services is an easy way to boost your online business.

Send Out a Newsletter (Either by E-mail or Mail)

Newsletters are an excellent way to keep customers interested in your products and services. The most important thing to remember about newsletters is that, in order for them to be effective, you must send them out regularly. If you send out a newsletter once or twice and then forget to send out another newsletter for a long time, your customers will forget about you, and you will have lost the advantage you gained from the first newsletters.

To create a mailing list for a mailed newsletter, ask people to sign up. If you want to get a bulk permit, you will need a minimum of 200 people, so you might need to send out a copy to family and friends in the beginning. Encourage people to sign up for the newsletter by including coupons or other incentives in it. Print sample copies and leave them for people to see as they visit your office. You will probably need someone to keep your mailing list up to date and to mail out the newsletters; this is a good part-time job for a teenager or stay-at-home parent.

To create a mailing list for your e-mail newsletter, put a link on your Web page. For online newsletters, it is best to find a mailing service who can handle enrollment and e-mailing the newsletter. Because of spam concerns, e-mail newsletters and other online senders are required to provide an "opt-out" to recipients. First, someone signs up for the newsletter. They receive an automatic reply that includes a link they must click or a box they must check, sending a reply back to the sender accepting the newsletter. On your e-mail newsletter, you also must include an "unsubscribe" box that allows recipients to stop getting your newsletter. Online newsletter services, like Constant Contact (**www.constantcontact.com**), can provide different levels of service as your e-mail newsletter list grows.

If you are wondering what to put in your e-mail newsletter, here are some suggestions about what to include:

- News of your industry and its affect on customers

- News about your company, such as new products, services, and hours

- Tips or advice relating to the kinds of products or services you provide. For a craft shop, for example, you could provide free online tips on how to do certain kinds of crafts.

- Seasonal information, tips, and creative shopping ideas

- Customer feedback or answers to customer questions

Once you begin writing your newsletter, you will find lots of possibilities to keep customers interested and, more importantly, to keep them coming back to your business for more purchases.

Offer Discounts

To entice new customers to your business, offering discounts is a common practice. A free introductory session with you for your services is a good example of a discount that will get people interested to see what your business is all about.

Some businesses offer regular discounts on seasonal merchandise, while others offer a discount as a reward to repeat customers. One common discount is the punch card, which customers bring each time to your business and have punched with each purchase. After so many purchases, they receive one of your products or services free or at a substantial reduction.

Take Advantage of the Internet

The Internet can be an extremely powerful marketing tool. Take every advantage of it that you can. Perhaps the best thing about the Internet is you can market your business, in many instances, for free or for very little.

Start a Blog

Blogs are the hottest thing on the Internet right now. Everyone from individuals who want to share their views with a large audience to big businesses that want to promote their products or services has a blog these days. You can create a free blog with one of the free online blogging services, such as WordPress or Blogger. The purpose of your blog is to create a community of people who will continue to come back for more and who will talk about your blog with other people.

To set up your blog, go to the blogging service and choose a template to set up the format for your blog. Then, begin blogging.

The best blogs are those that encourage reader comments. Ranting and preaching will not be as effective in gaining you loyal blog readers as asking for opinions or bringing up interesting ideas and asking for comments. Be sure to create an "About" section on your blog so readers can find out more about your background and experience.

Create Online Articles

To establish your credentials as an expert in your field, try your hand at writing online articles. Give advice to people who might want to buy your products or services, and send your article to an online service like **www .submityourarticle.com**. If the service approves your article, it will get picked up by a number of online article sites and get distributed to people who want to read about your subject. Writing an online article is also a good way to get your expertise recognized by people who might hire you for work, since you can include a short biography at the end of your article to describe your background and credentials or to promote your latest work.

Sign Up for Online Directories

More and more people are using the Internet to find local and online businesses, and they use directories like Google Local for this purpose. Like local Yellow Pages advertising, there are many online directories where you can get your business Web site listed. Some of these list for free, and most allow you the opportunity to pay for a higher-level listing. For example, Google Local allows local businesses to pay for a top advertiser listing, in addition to the regular alphabetical listing. The Yellow Pages companies, such as Dex, also have online directories to help people find local and national businesses providing products and services.

Join Link Exchanges

Another good way to get your business recognized and visited online is to join forces with others who are advertising to the same market. In this instance, joining forces means exchanging links with the other advertisers between your blogs and Web sites. For example, if your specialty paper business has a Web site, you can find others who might advertise to the people who buy specialty paper (maybe a specialty pen business) and e-mail that business to ask about exchanging links. An additional value to this exchange is that Google and other search engines look for sites that have many links to other sites, so these links will improve your ranking and move you up the list when people go to the Web to find your service.

Incorporate Podcasting and Video Ads

With the advent of YouTube and other video sites, many companies are considering advertising by video. In order to do this advertising online, you will need to create a compelling and interesting video ad and find some way to put it on a digital video. You can purchase a digital video through a Webcam on your computer, or you can find someone with a digital video camera to record your online ad. Placing your ad on a free Web service such as YouTube is easy. After you have placed your ad online, link it to your blog or Web site or place it directly on your site. People love to watch short videos, and they are an excellent way for you to provide more explanation about your product or service than people can get by reading.

Use Testimonials

People buy products and services that are recommended by other people. Looking on television, for example, you can find many instances where people are saying, "Buy this. I tried it, and it works." One of the most effective methods for selling your product or service is to show testimonials from people who have good things to say to your potential customers. Here are some suggestions for getting and using testimonials:

- **The best testimonials are unsolicited.** If someone tries your product or service and says, "Wow! This is great," ask if he or she would mind putting that in writing. Make it easy for him or her to write down or put his or her comments on video. You will find that people love to tell people what to do, and they will not hesitate to agree if you ask.

- **You must get a release for all testimonials**, either before the actual testimonial is received or immediately after. Have a release form ready for people to sign or e-mail back to someone who agrees to do a testimonial. The release should state simply that the person agrees to allow your business to use his or her name, face, and other information supplied for the purpose of advertising and promoting your business. The release also should include an acknowledgement that the person is not receiving any reimbursement or payment for this release.

- **When someone does a testimonial for your business, let the person tell his or her story in his or her own words.** Edit as little as possible. The most powerful testimonials are un-coached and non-professional. Changing words to make them as you want can destroy the spontaneity and folksiness of the testimonial.

- **Change your testimonials frequently.** People get used to seeing a testimonial and pay little attention to it. If you have a business where people come in frequently, such as a hair salon, you can put up photos of satisfied customers (after getting their release, of course), and change those photos every month or so.

Make the Most of Your E-mail Signature Line

Using every opportunity to tell people about your business is the hallmark of an effective business person. So using your e-mail signature to sell is a great idea. Certainly you will want to include your name and contact information, but also include a logo or photo and a catchphrase that describes your business.

Like all your advertising and promotions, you should change your signature line often, to keep it fresh and get people to notice it again. Include your latest promotion, a holiday offer, or just a different look. Tell people to go to your Web site for more information and include a direct link to the purchase of your product or service.

Join Online Forums

For every type of business, there is probably a group of people online chatting about it. Professional freelance writers, for example, have many online forums where they gather to talk about issues relating to their profession. Find and get involved in an online forum. Use it as a way to gain information about pricing, tips on new ways to attract clients, and advice on how to deal with clients. Some forums allow you to advertise, using pay-per-click advertising.

If your type of business has an online forum for customers, that is an even better place to frequent and advertise. You can offer advice to customers and get your professional credentials enhanced by your presence in such venues. Be careful not to spend too much time in these forums, though, at the expense of other promotional activities.

chapter 9

All About Self-Employed Taxes

Now that you are self-employed, you must consider the tax implications of your business, and you must set up a system to be sure that you pay your business taxes on time. This section is a review of the business taxes that must be paid. The assumption in this section is that you are a sole proprietor working alone.

If you are the owner of a C corporation, the corporation pays taxes on its corporate income, and you pay taxes as an employee. If you are a member of an LLC or if your business is set up as an S corporation, you can elect to pay taxes as a sole proprietor. In these cases, most of the discussion below will apply to you.

Business or Hobby

Be aware that the IRS will be concerned about whether your business is a true business and not a hobby. If your business involves activities that might be considered hobbies, such as woodworking, crafts, or collecting stamps or coins, you will need to show that you are operating as a business in order to deduct your business expenses. Some of the ways you can show that you are operating as a business are:

- Do you keep good business records?

- Do you operate with the intention of making a profit?

- Have you made a profit on this activity in the past? If not, is there expectation that you will make a profit in the future?

- Do you have the skill, education, and experience to operate the business successfully?

The ABCs of Paying Taxes as a Self-Employed Person (Self-Employment Taxes)

Self-employed individuals, as stated above, pay tax on their business income through their personal income tax return. Your business income tax is calculated using the Schedule C that is part of Form 1040 (the personal tax return form). The total net income from Schedule C is added to your personal tax return as one line of income, along with your other income. Schedule C asks for the following information:

- Gross receipts (sales) from all sources

- Cost of goods sold. You will have to determine how much it cost you to produce the products you have sold.

- Inventory of unsold goods

From these numbers, you will come up with a total gross sales figure for the year. Then you are asked to list totals for all deductible expenses for the year. These expenses include:

- Advertising

- Supplies

- Taxes and licenses

- Travel

- Meals and entertainment (at 50 percent)

- Car and truck expenses, including mileage

- Commissions and fees

- Depreciation

- Employee benefit programs

- Utilities

- Insurance

- Wages

- Interest on loans and mortgages

- Legal and professional services

The final item in the Schedule C is "Net Income," the result of subtracting total expenses from gross sales. The net income figure is important, because this is what your tax liability is based on.

Paying Self-Employment Taxes

In addition to your liability to pay taxes on your business's net income, as a self-employed individual you also must pay self-employment taxes for Social Security and Medicare. This calculation is also part of the 1040 form and is also based on the net income from your business.

The self-employment tax rate for 2007 is 15.3 percent, up to a total of $97,500. If your net business income is $100,000, you have to pay $15,300. This payment is required in addition to your personal income tax and is paid at the same time you pay your taxes.

Paying Taxes

Employees of businesses are required to pay taxes on their income each pay period, based on the estimated tax they will pay each year. As a self-employed individual, you do not have a salary from which income tax may be withheld; therefore, the IRS requires you to make estimated quarterly tax payments.

You will have to estimate your income for the year, based on your income from previous years, and make payments directly to the IRS. If this is your first year in business, your accountant may ask you to make estimated payments so your tax bill at the end of the year is not too high and to avoid any penalties for underpayment.

Reducing Your Taxes

The purpose of the detailed list of expenses is to show you what kinds of items you should be keeping track of in order to reduce your taxes. You should be claiming all these items as deductible expenses, but in order to do so, you must have documentation of your business expenditures. For example, in order to claim mileage you must be able to prove the expense. If you are audited, you must be able to show the date or dates, the mileage driven, and the specific business purpose.

Keeping good business records can protect you in the event of an IRS audit. These records can help you answer questions about whether you have a hobby and how much profit you made for the year. If you do not have records, you might have to pay late fees and penalties on your income.

1099 Forms

If you are an independent contractor who has been paid more than $600 during any year, you will receive a 1099-Miscellaneous form from your customer, which you must include in your income. Each 1099 must be recorded separately, because a duplicate copy is sent to the IRS, which may want to track your income from these sources.

In return, if you have an independent contractor working for you, you must prepare and file a 1099 for that person for the year, no later than February 28 of the following year. Note that you do not have to file a 1099 if the contractor is a corporation.

Tips for Finding an Accountant

In the course of taking care of the finances of your business, you will need to hire several kinds of financial advisory services. You may be able to find these services together in one business. The services you will need include:

- **Bookkeeping.** Unless you elect to do your bookkeeping internally, you will need someone to keep your business books on a spreadsheet or accounting software program each month.

- **Accounting.** An accountant is an individual who can help you set up your financial records and review them monthly, quarterly, and annually.

- **Certified public accountant.** A CPA is an individual with the credentials and experience to advise you about tax matters and to represent you before the IRS in the event of an audit.

- **Tax advisor.** A tax advisor can review your books and give you advice about how to reduce your taxes.

These duties overlap to a great extent. If you can find an accounting firm that provides bookkeeping services and includes a CPA as well as an individual who operates as a tax advisor, this would be the best solution for your financial needs.

When searching for an accountant, try to find one who has experience with the specific type of business you are operating. Some accountants specialize in certain kinds of businesses. For example, if you have an online business, you should find someone who has knowledge of online financial operations. The best way to find someone is to ask others in your business field. Note that, while you may be able to find an online bookkeeper, you will probably need a local CPA to talk to about tax issues.

Paying Sales Taxes

If you are selling a product or a service for which sales tax is due, you will need to follow the requirements of your state in setting up and paying sales taxes. For online sales, you also must follow state requirements. At the present time, most businesses do not collect sales tax on Internet transactions with individuals outside the state in which the business is operating, but this might change.

For most states, you are required to charge the appropriate amount of sales tax for the location in which your business is operating. This tax includes state, county, and local option taxes. You also are required to report all sales and to pay sales tax collected to the state on a regular basis. Many states allow you to pay and report sales taxes online. Check online for the state regulations at the department of revenue for your state.

CASE STUDY: JUNE WALKER

June Walker always has preferred working for herself. As a young woman, she pursued several self-employed ventures. Although each pursuit was unique, there was a common thread. In every instance, whatever the situation, tax consultants and accountants lacked an understanding and competence in dealing with a solo entrepreneur.

The problem was not just her own. While working for an industrial design company, she found that the skilled technical consultants with whom she dealt were getting unskilled tax advice. As an artists' representative, she saw that artists were equally in need of sound tax guidance. The entire self-employed sector of the economy, she came to realize, was not being properly served.

With enormous respect for the talents and imagination of the independent professional, Walker called upon her math, science, business, financial, and artistic experience to develop an accounting practice that would educate the self-employed about the business side of their endeavors. Today her clientele is composed exclusively of the self-employed, or, as she calls them, "indies."

In the 25 years since she started her business, she has sought to disseminate accurate, easy-to-understand, simply written tax and recordkeeping advice to an ever-growing indie population. Walker expanded her reach by writing for magazines, presenting seminars and workshops, becoming an author (her highly praised book, *Self-employed Tax Solutions*, is now in its 6th printing) and using the Internet, her Web site (**www.junewalkeronline.com**), and her blog (**http://junewalkeronline.blogspot.com**) to further her educational project.

Upfront, irreverent, and flexible, Walker is an independent spirit who does not fit the accountant stereotype. She is an advocate of simplicity, order, and ease in dealing with tax laws that are complex, confusing, and unfair to indies. She has developed her own simple method for gathering and recording tax and financial information. She imparts to indies a clear understanding of how to make the tax laws and regulations work for their solo enterprises.

Before relocating in 1995 to Santa Fe, New Mexico, Walker maintained offices in New York and New Jersey. Her clients, more than 200 in number, live throughout the United States, Canada, and Europe.

How Long to Keep Tax Records

Tax expert June Walker gives some advice on keeping tax records.

ADVICE ON KEEPING TAX RECORDS

Contrary to popular opinion, people don't usually get into trouble by not saving records but by saving the wrong ones, outdated ones, and too many or by not knowing where the right ones are. The huge stack of papers in the attic is often there due to inertia caused by not knowing which records need to be kept and which can be tossed. Here's a quick guide.

Record Retention Simply Stated

- Keep tax returns (not records but actual returns) forever.

Label a box **MY TAX RETURNS** and put them in there.

- Keep every year-end summary of your pension forever.

Label a box **PENSIONS** and make a folder for each plan you have. Put that plan's year-end statement in the folder and close the box.

- Keep everything else for seven years from the last time it had any impact on your financial life.

For instance, label a box **2007 TAX RECORDS: OK to throw out 12/31/2014**.

How Long to Keep Records

Although most audits take place within two years from the time you file your return, if you unknowingly (that is, not intentionally) neglect to include at least 25% of your income on your return, the statute of limitations is extended from three years after filing to six years after filing. That's seven years from the time of the transaction. For instance, your 2007 tax return is filed in 2008.

HOW LONG TO KEEP RECORDS

The Record	The Situation	Keep Records for How Long
TAX RETURNS	Any	Forever
RECORDS SUBSTANTIATING YOUR TAX RETURN	Filed on time, including extensions	Seven years from the year of the transactions
	Filed late	Six years from filing date
	Paid late	Six years from last payment
	Filed a fraudulent return	Forever
	Never filed a return	Forever
RECEIPTS FOR A MULTIYEAR DEDUCTION	Any	Seven years after the year you disposed of it

ADVICE ON KEEPING TAX RECORDS

Tossing With Assurance

As Walker says, people don't usually get into trouble by not saving records but by saving the wrong ones. Don't confuse keeping records with never throwing out a piece of paper.

Use the table on page 212 as a guide for pitching to the round file with assurance, but do remember there are other personal business records not included in this table. These include:

- Birth and death certificates
- Marriage and divorce papers
- Adoption papers
- Military service records
- Wills
- Asset lists — so your estate can be properly administered
- Medical records
- Loan and lease agreements
- Personal and business insurance policies
- Active warranties and service contracts on equipment
- Employment agreements
- Pension documents
- Records of pension contributions and withdrawals
- Pension forms 5500 or 5500-EZ

Keep these records, each in its own file folder, clearly labeled, in a safe place.

© Copyright 2007. June Walker.

chapter 10

Easy Recordkeeping and Accounting

Your ability to keep track of your financial records is critical to the success of your business. You need to be able to track income and expenditures, both for your own purposes and for tax reporting.

Before you begin your business, you must make several decisions about how you will run the financial part of your business, including these:

- What accounting period you will use

- Whether you will run your business on a cash or an accrual basis

- What accounts to set up for recording transactions

- What records to keep and for how long

- What financial reporting program to use

- Whether to do your bookkeeping yourself or hire a bookkeeper

- What accounting and tax service provider to use

Several of these decisions need to be made immediately, because they relate to questions you will be asked when you fill out your initial business applications. Others will need to be made as soon as you start your business.

Begin by keeping proper financial records. It is much easier to do it right the first time than to catch up with the financial part of your business later.

You can begin doing your own bookkeeping, but you may find that the time spent on financial concerns takes you away from your clients and reduces your ability to make money. Depending on your hourly rate, it may make sense for you to start out with a bookkeeping service.

Accounting Periods

The accounting period of your business is called the fiscal year. Most small businesses use the calendar year (from January 1 to December 31) as their fiscal year. If you are a sole proprietorship, this is the best accounting period to use, since you are filing your personal income taxes for the calendar year. If you are in an LLC or a Subchapter S corporation, you should also use the calendar year as your business fiscal year, since you will be passing your taxes on to your personal tax return. Your town or city probably will have a bookkeeping service you can talk to, or you might want to try an online bookkeeping service.

If you are organized as a C corporation or if you are an LLC choosing to be taxed as a corporation, you can choose any fiscal year that makes sense. Some businesses are cyclical, having high-sales and low-sales periods, and often choose the low-sales period as their fiscal year end. This gives them time to finalize their books and file taxes.

You will need to decide on your fiscal year before you start your business, since you will be asked this question on several startup forms, including the SS-4 application for an Employer ID Number.

Cash Versus Accrual Accounting

Small businesses use one of two bookkeeping systems to record sales and expenses: cash or accrual accounting. You will be required to check either "cash" or "accrual" on your application for an Employer ID number and on your tax return each year. Which you use is important at the end of the fiscal year, as it determines in what year you should record a sale or an expense.

The simplest method, and the one most small businesses use, is cash accounting. In this type of accounting, income is recorded when the payment is received, and expenses are recorded when they are paid. For a business that does not have a long time between invoicing and receipt, this is the easiest method to use. If you invoice a client on December 1 and receive payment on January 15, the sale is recorded on January 15, not in December. If you pay in December, however, the expense can be used for your tax reporting in that year. This can be an advantage to small businesses that want to reduce their net income and tax payments.

In accrual accounting, on the other hand, a sale is recorded when the client is invoiced, and an expense is recorded when the bill is received. Cash does not need to change hands for there to be a recordable transaction. If there is a long time between invoicing and payment, you may use the accrual method. For example, under the accrual system, if you issue an invoice to a client on December 1, even if client is not expected to pay until February 1, the sale is recorded in December.

The cash method is used by most sole proprietors and by other small businesses that are not selling products. If you are selling a product, you will have inventory of products, parts, or materials that you have paid for and are waiting to sell. You usually must pay for the inventory at the time you receive it.

Larger businesses with annual sales in excess of $5 million, as well as publicly traded companies, are required to use accrual accounting, because this method complies with the requirements of the Securities and Exchange Commission and with Generally Accepted Accounting Principles. As a small business that does not sell products, you may not be required to use accrual accounting; however, check with your accountant to be sure.

Simple Bookkeeping Procedures

The type of bookkeeping used by most businesses, small and large, is called double-entry bookkeeping. It is based on the principle of keeping everything in balance. If the books are out of balance, it is easy to recognize and find errors quickly.

Every financial activity in a business is a transaction, including a sales transaction, payment of your rent, buying a computer, or paying a monthly amount on your business credit card. Even the smallest transaction is important, because these transactions represent the financial activity of your business. Neglecting to record every transaction means you are not recording your business activity. In addition, if you fail to record every expense transaction, you lose the benefit of legitimate tax reductions.

If you travel 20 miles to a client site and you do this every weekday for six weeks, you have traveled 600 miles. Given the IRS-allowable rate of 48 cents per mile, if you do not record the cost for these trips, that is a $288 business expense that you cannot count on your tax return. The little transactions may not seem like much, but they add up.

Setting Up Your Bookkeeping System

Before you can record transactions, you need to set up a bookkeeping system.

To begin, set up a "Chart of Accounts" by designating specific accounts to be used for recording transactions. These accounts are set up in five categories:

- **Category 1:** Assets, which are items your business owns that have value. Assets are listed in order of liquidity, which relates to how quickly they can be turned into cash.

- **Category 2:** Liabilities, which are amounts you owe to others, either on a long-term or on a short-term basis. Liabilities are listed according to how quickly they must be paid off.

- **Category 3:** Income, which is listed by the types of products and services you sell. This category also includes accounts for returns and adjustments to sales, which reduce the total sales. If you are selling products, this category will include "Cost of Goods Sold," which is either the wholesale price you paid for the product or the cost of the items you used to make the product.

- **Category 4:** Expenses, or the amounts you owe to others on a continual basis. This category comprises the largest number of accounts, and it is the area where you will need to make the most decisions about how many accounts to include.

- **Category 5:** Owner's equity shows the net amount you own of the business. Owner's equity is determined by calculating the company's net worth, which is the total assets less the total liabilities of the company.

For example, if a business has $500,000 in assets and $300,000 in liabilities, its net worth is $200,000. Net worth also takes into account the profits of the business over the preceding periods of time, so it represents the increasing or decreasing value of the owner's equity (ownership) in the business.

Determining which accounts to include in the Chart of Accounts is an important decision, because what you record is shown on your reports at the end of each month, each quarter, and each year. If you do not record something, you will not have the full information about your business for your own personal use or for tax purposes.

Consider how much detail you want to know about your business before you begin. For example, do you want to know the amount you spend on each utility (e.g., gas, electric, phone, water, and sewage) separately, or can you list them all together? The more detail you include, in the form of separate accounts, the more information you have at your disposal.

This is a list of all the accounts you might need in order to keep track of financial records:

1. Assets

   a. Cash

      i. In your business checking account

      ii. In your payroll account if you are paying employees

      iii. In business savings or money market accounts

      iv. On hand in your office for paying small amounts ("petty cash")

   b. Receivables, which are amounts owed to your business by others

   c. Inventories, if you are selling products

      i. Finished goods for sale

      ii. Work in process

      iii. Raw materials

  d. Prepaid expenses. These are amounts you have paid before they are due.

      i. The most common prepaid expenses are for insurance and advertising, which you may pay in advance for several months at a time. There is a value in these amounts because you are able to get a refund if you cancel the policy or the advertising.

      ii. You also may have prepaid rent, usually in the form of a security deposit on which you can get a refund if you leave.

  e. Property and equipment

      i. Land, which has a separate value from the building

      ii. Buildings, listed at purchase price

      iii. Allowance for depreciation, which reduces the asset value of the building

      iv. Automobiles and trucks, if these are the property of the business and are used for business purposes. These assets are listed at purchase price.

      v. Allowance for depreciation on autos and trucks

      vi. Furniture and office equipment, listed at purchase price

      vii. Allowance for depreciation on each item of furniture and office equipment

      viii. Leasehold improvements (sometimes called "build-out" by real estate people), which are improvements you have made to an office or building to make it usable for your business. These improvements may include constructing walls, adding lighting fixtures and outlets, renovating restrooms, and other construction.

      ix. Allowance for depreciation on leasehold improvements

2.   Liabilities

   a. Notes and accounts payable to others. These liabilities, listed as "payables," are short-term amounts representing bills you have received and that you have not paid at the time the report is produced.

   b. Current payables on long-term debts. These are amounts payable within the next year on long-term debts, such as loans and mortgages.

3.   Owner's equity

   a. An equity account for each owner or partner. Amounts are held separately for each individual who is eligible to receive a share of the profits of the business. If you are a sole proprietor, you receive the entire net income of the business. If you are in a partnership, a shareholder of a corporation, or a member of an LLC, your share of the net income is distributed to your equity account according to the written terms of the agreement in place.

   b. A draw account for each owner or partner. Draw accounts represent amounts taken out from the business by owners or partners for personal use. Draws reduce the amount of equity (ownership) of the individual. For example, if your equity account as a sole proprietor as of the date of the report is $50,000 and you have drawn out $5,000 for personal use, your net equity is $45,000.

For a business that is organized as a corporation, this section is listed as "Shareholder's Equity," and the section includes an account for "Retained Earnings." The retained earnings are income amounts held by the company for growth and development, rather than paying these amounts to the shareholders in the form of dividends. There is no draw account for a corporation, because amounts are paid out only in the form of pay to employees or dividends to shareholders.

4. Income

    a. Sales of merchandise and services. You may have several different accounts in this section, representing various products and/or services you sell. For example, if you are selling several categories of products, you may want to list each specifically. A wine vendor may want to record sales of domestic wines separately from foreign wines and may even want to break down wine sales by vineyard or distributor. The possibilities for recording sales are limited only by your interest in knowing where your sales are coming from.

    b. Sales returns and allowance. You will need to record returns and allowances as negative totals in this section. Reductions to sales will reduce your tax liability.

    c. Cash discounts allowed to customers. In the same way as sales returns, you will want to record discounts as reductions to sales. If you do not record these reductions, your sales figures will be higher than actual sales.

    d. Cost of goods sold. If your business is selling products, you will need to keep track of the amounts that were spent on buying the products from a wholesaler or for the materials and supplies used to create the products. A quilt shop, for example, records its cost for bolts of fabric that it sells to customers and also records the cost of time and materials in producing quilts for resale. Recording everything that goes into a product you sell can be tedious, but the IRS requires that you go through this exercise so you can include "Cost of Goods Sold" on your business tax return each year. If you are selling a product, you will need an accountant to help you set up a process for determining costs of goods sold.

5. Expenses

   a. Operating expenses

      i. Wages and salaries paid to employees (gross amounts)

      ii. Supplies. Depending on the type of business you have, you will want to keep separate categories for different kinds of supplies, such as office supplies, production supplies, and maintenance supplies.

      iii. Equipment rental. If you are renting both office equipment and equipment related to making a product, you will need to keep these kinds of equipment in separate categories.

      iv. Repairs and maintenance on equipment.

   b. Selling expenses

      i. Advertising expenses

      ii. Expenses relating to salespeople, such as travel expenses

      iii. Commissions on sales

       iv. Entertainment of clients

c. Administrative expenses. This category includes everything you need to run your office.

       i. Office supplies, if these are kept separate from other supplies

       ii. Postage

       iii. Phones

       iv. Dues and subscriptions to trade publications or professional journals

       v. Insurance

       vi. Professional services, for your attorney and CPA, and for any other professionals who work as independent contractors and provide specific services to your business, such as a virtual assistant or business coach.

       vii. Automobile expenses, if you are using your car for business purposes. It is important that you separate expenses for driving back and forth to work (which are not considered business expenses) from legitimate business use of your car, such as for calls on clients or to professional meetings.

       viii. Bad debts. This category is set up to allow you to delete any uncollected accounts receivable at the end of each year. You will need to work with your accountant to determine whether there are any clients who you expect will never pay you; the amounts these clients owe can be deducted legitimately from your profits each year before you pay taxes.

   ix. Building expenses

     1. Rent on your office space or building

     2. Utilities, including gas, electric, water, and sewage

     3. Maintenance expenses, such as snow removal, landscaping services, and lawn mowing services

     4. Building repairs

   x. Depreciation, including decreases in the value of buildings and other assets over time

   xi. Taxes paid

     1. Payroll taxes, such as FICA (Social Security and Medicare), federal and state unemployment, and workers' compensation taxes

     2. Real estate taxes on any buildings owned by your business

     3. Federal income taxes paid on behalf of the business

     4. State income taxes paid on behalf of the business

Recording Business Depreciation

All assets have a built-in decrease in value, called "depreciation." Recording depreciation is an important process for small businesses, because depreciation is an expense, and expenses reduce net income for tax purposes. Depreciation is important in business accounting, because if it is not included in the calculations of business ownership, the value of the business's assets is not accurate. While your business may have a computer that you purchased for $2,000 three years ago, it does not have a value of $2,000 today.

There are two kinds of depreciation: functional and obsolescence. Assets depreciate functionally because they lose their usefulness; they do not work as well as they once did. A good example of that is a car, which needs more maintenance and repairs as it gets older. Assets also depreciate by becoming obsolete, because newer models are produced that take their place. Cars again are a good example, because this year's model makes last year's model less valuable.

Depreciation is calculated by dividing the purchase price of an asset by its estimated useful life, less its salvage (scrap) value. The result is an annual depreciation on the asset. For example, say you purchased a desk for your business and paid $1,000 for it. The desk has a useful life of nine years and a scrap value of $100. The net value of the desk is its purchase price less the scrap value, which is $900. Each year for the nine years of its useful life, you can deduct $100 in expenses for your business.

Recording depreciation on business assets is important to reduce income for tax purposes and to accurately reflect the current value of each asset over time. It is important to remember that depreciation has nothing to do with how the asset was purchased. It may have been bought with a credit card or cash or paid for as part of a business startup loan. The depreciation calculation is completely independent of the purchase of the asset.

Calculating the useful life for each type of business asset is done by the IRS. A CPA is an invaluable resource in helping you with the necessary depreciation calculations. Typically these calculations are part of the final preparations for paying business taxes, so you do not need to worry about them, except for keeping track of purchase prices.

Business Reports

The value of all these accounts becomes clear when you put the information together into business reports. For small businesses, two reports are produced for the business on a monthly, quarterly, and annual basis.

Balance sheet. The first report is a balance sheet, which combines information on assets, liabilities, and owner's equity into a single statement showing the "state of the business" at a single date. This date is usually the end of the period in question. For example, an end-of-year balance sheet for a business might be titled:

Balance Sheet
Cosgrove Quilt Shop
As of December 31, 2007

Traditionally, assets are listed in the left column with cash first and other assets listed in the order in which they quickly could be turned into cash. Equipment assets are listed along with allowances for depreciation for each asset.

Liabilities are listed on the right side of the balance sheet, in the order of time by which they must be paid – shortest time to longest time.

Owner's equity or shareholder's equity accounts are listed under liabilities on the right. The total of the liabilities and owner's equity amounts on the right must equal the total assets on the left.

Income statement. While the balance sheet summarizes the state of the business at a moment in time, the income statement shows the activity, in terms of sales and expenses, of the business over a length of time. The income statement includes information about the income of the business from sales of products and services, less returns, allowances, and discounts, and costs of products sold. It also records information on the expenses of the business over that same length of time.

The traditional way to set up an income statement is to show income first, by category of sales. Then expenses are listed, along with calculations of their percentage of sales. The net income of the business for that time period is listed last.

Reading and Evaluating Business Reports

As you produce your balance sheets and income statements for your business, you must evaluate these reports over time and make note of what has changed.

Looking at the balance sheet for one month, you might not be able to see much; however, if you look at the balance sheet for the current month in comparison to the month before, you can see if your cash balances have increased, if your liabilities have decreased, and if your owner's equity has gone up. You may want to view these reports on a quarterly and yearly basis, rather than month by month, since in most businesses there are cycles that fluctuate over time and that might give you a false negative or positive picture of the business.

Looking at the income statement for one quarter compared to the income statement for the previous quarter, pay close attention in particular to these sections:

1. Sales by category of product and service. What categories of products or services increased? What categories decreased? Following these trends might lead you to make changes in your sales offerings.

2. Expenses as a percentage of sales. Keeping close track of expenses is a key to good business practices. If you see that one category of expenses is increasing as a percentage of sales, this might be an indication that

those expenses are unruly and might need to be limited. If advertising is increasing as a percentage of sales, this might mean that you have initiated an advertising campaign, but if sales increase as a result, the increased advertising expense might not be a negative.

Running periodic balance sheet and income statement reports is good business practice. Your CPA probably will ask for these reports at least on a quarterly basis, and you should make a practice of talking with him or her at least once a quarter to discuss potential tax implications of your business activity.

Recording Financial Transactions

When you have set up your Chart of Accounts at the beginning of your business, you then will need to begin keeping track of transactions on a daily basis. The best way to keep track of transactions is to capture them as they happen and record them periodically.

Capture them as they happen.

- If you are traveling, keep an envelope or small pocket file folder in your car and put receipts in it as you get them.

- If you receive bills in the mail, keep them in a file folder on your desk after you pay them.

- Print out copies of client invoices.

- Keep copies of checks you receive, as well as PayPal or other online receipts.

Record them periodically. Every month, go through all these financial documents and record the information from each into a bookkeeping program or Excel worksheet. For each document record the date, the amount, whom the transaction was to or from, and what it was for. For the information to be most useful, include the specific account affected by the transaction. For example, if you purchase postage stamps with cash, note "Postage" when you record the transaction.

Popular Bookkeeping Software

If you are considering doing your books yourself, look at some of the most popular business accounting software packages. Among these are QuickBooks® and Peachtree®. These programs are useful if you want to pay employees, make payroll reports, write checks, send invoices directly to clients, and record cost of goods sold for products. They also can help you keep track of clients with invoices and sales receipts, and they allow you to produce accounts receivable reports.

If your business is very small, you might consider setting up an Excel spreadsheet for recording this information. You also can use an online accounting program to set up your books and produce accounting reports. Your data are stored online on the server of the provider. Some of these services also include online marketing and merchant services, so they are worth looking into if you are considering an online business.

Paying Taxes on and for Employees

If your business has employees, you will need to keep good records on taxes deducted from their paychecks and to pay these taxes to the appropriate federal and state agencies. Paying payroll taxes can be complicated, and you should get the advice of your tax advisor when setting up payroll systems.

For all employees, federal law requires the following:

1. **W-4 form.** The first thing you need to do when hiring an employee

is to have that person fill out a W-4 form designating the way he or she wants federal income tax deducted from each pay. You will use the W-4 form to help you calculate the amount of the employee's deduction, which depends on the number of deductions and the amount of the paycheck.

2. **Per-pay deductions.** From each employee paycheck you will need to make several deductions:

   a. Income tax, based on the calculations from the W-4 form and depending on the amount of the person's paycheck

   b. Social Security and Medicare deductions, calculated at 7.65 percent of the gross amount of the person's paycheck up to a specified maximum amount for Social Security (but not Medicare) each year. For 2007, for example, the Social Security maximum is $97,500.

3. **Payables from payroll.** After you have calculated the total deductions for all employees for each payroll, you must set aside amounts equal to the following:

   a. The total for all income tax deductions you made from employee paychecks.

   b. The total Social Security and Medicare deductions you made from employee paychecks.

   c. The total Social Security and Medicare deductions for this payroll. This amount is required to be paid by you as the employer for each employee's Social Security and Medicare.

4. **Paying employment taxes.** Depending on the number of employees and the total payroll, you will need to make payments to the IRS

on either a monthly or a quarterly basis of the amounts you have set aside (Item 3 at left) from employee paychecks and from your business funds. Failure to pay these amounts can result in fines and penalties, so it is important that you remember to make these payments or have your tax advisor remind you when these payments are due.

5. **Payroll reporting.** At the end of each quarter, you must complete a report to the IRS providing information on the amounts you owe to the IRS for employee Social Security and Medicare and showing the amounts you have deducted from employee paychecks for income tax and Social Security/Medicare. You also must show the amounts paid to the IRS from these accounts. If the amount paid is less than the amount owed, you must send in the difference; if it is more than the amount owed, you can get credit against your next payment. As with the payment of taxes, failure to file these reports in a timely manner can lead to fines and penalties being imposed on your business.

6. **Paying unemployment taxes.** In addition to the taxes described above, employers are required to make payments (either on a monthly or on a quarterly basis) into a federal unemployment tax fund. These payments are approximately 0.8 percent of the total gross amount of each payroll (for all employees). You cannot deduct money from employees for this fund; it must come from your business funds. You also must file a report showing the amounts owed and paid for this fund.

7. **Workers' compensation.** You must pay into a federal workers' compensation fund for all employees, based on your gross payroll and a rate determined by the type of company you have.

8. **Year-end reporting.** After the end of each year, you are required to send each employee a statement of earnings and deductions for the

last year on a W-2 form and to send a form to the IRS showing the total deductions for income tax and Social Security/Medicare for all employees, along with a copy of each employee's W-2 form.

Of course, these are just the most common federal payroll taxes that all businesses with employees must pay and report. Other taxes you may have to collect from employees and/or pay from your company's funds are:

1. *State income taxes.* These amounts are calculated from the federal W-4 form, deducted from employee paychecks, and paid to the state where your business is located.

2. *State unemployment taxes.* You must pay these amounts based on gross payroll for all employees at a rate specified by your state.

If you have more than a few employees, keeping records, making payments, and providing payroll information can be almost a full-time job. As a business owner, you must be prepared for an auditor who will examine your payroll records to be certain you are properly calculating deductions and providing information to employees with each payroll. As your business grows, it might be a good idea to use the services of a payroll processing company, either a local business or an online service, to be sure you are in compliance with the law.

chapter 11

Writing and Using Client Agreements

If you are working as an independent contractor providing services for clients, you will need to prepare and use a client agreement form. The purpose of this agreement is to set out the expectations and goals of both the client and the provider, to lessen the chances of issues that might damage the relationship between the parties, and to set out ways to resolve issues that might arise.

Work for Hire

The concept of work for hire is important to understand before you enter into any client agreements. According to the basic principles of copyright law, any work produced by an individual is owned by that individual. An exception is the case of work for hire, which is when an individual produces a work for someone else with the understanding that the buyer owns all rights to that work. The contractor may not assert any ownership of the work and may not put his or her name on the work as author. Of course, the work-for-hire agreement involves the payment of a reasonable amount for that work.

In a work-for-hire arrangement, you are agreeing to get paid to produce something for someone else and for which that other person or entity will take credit. In most cases, the client asserts all right to the work in all media. For example, if you are producing a book, you cannot own movie or video rights to that book. Such arrangements are commonplace in such fields as computer software design, freelance writing, and graphic art.

There is a variety of possibilities in work-for-hire agreements. For example, the client may be willing to allow you to take credit for or use a work after a certain time period or in certain media. You also may be able to obtain coauthor rights with someone else for a work in return for a lesser price for your services.

If the client prepares the work-for-hire agreement, you can attempt to negotiate any part of that agreement. You may find the client firm in some areas and amenable to changes in others. One example is the case above, where you receive some co-ownership of the work in return for a lesser price. You also may be able to take back ownership of the work after a period of time.

Provisions of a Client Agreement

Here is the breakdown of a typical work-for-hire or client agreement:

1. **Nature of the assignment/description of work.** This section details what work is to be done by the contractor. It also describes both parties in the agreement, including their legal form of business.

2. **Delivery and acceptance of work.** This section describes how the work is to be delivered to the client (e.g., by e-mail or in printed form) and the timeline in which the work is to be done.

3. **Consideration/payment.** This section may be included with the previous section, and it lays out the schedule of payments.

4. **Independent contractor status.** The independent contractor

relationship is described, so it is clear the contractor is not an employee.

5. **Trade secrets / confidentiality / proprietary information.** Sometimes called an NDA (non-disclosure agreement), this section states that the contractor agrees not to reveal proprietary information about the client or trade secrets and that the contractor will not breach the confidentiality of the client.

6. **Representations and warranties.** Usually this section applies to the contractor, who represents that the work being produced is original and has not been plagiarized.

7. **Governing law.** The contract is stated to conform to the laws of a specific state, usually the state in which the client is located.

It is possible to prepare your own client agreement, but you might want to have your attorney prepare a general form that you can modify later for different clients. Some clients have their own forms. If the client's form is similar to your form, you may decide to sign it. If it is unfamiliar or if you have major concerns about a portion of the agreement, check with your attorney. Do not hesitate to turn down an agreement if the client refuses to change a part of the agreement that you find problematic.

Nondisclosure Agreements

The provisions of the nondisclosure agreement (NDA) are essential to the concept of work for hire. An NDA might be part of a client agreement, as in the listing of terms above, or you may be presented with a separate NDA before you begin work.

NDAs are used in business situations in which the project requires that confidential, proprietary, or trade secret information be shared with the contractor. For example, if you are contracted to write a business plan, you will need the financial projections of the company. The following is a list of some other types of information that might be the subject of an NDA: pending litigation; marketing plans; proprietary processes or systems in a company; copyright, patent, or trademark information; and unpublished works.

An NDA protects a client against the eventuality that a contractor will disclose company information to outsiders. It also serves as notice to the contractor of the consequences of disclosing this information, either intentionally or unintentionally. Finally, the NDA provides for the process by which a lawsuit is carried out in the event of a breach of this agreement.

If you are conducting your own business and you have information that you do not wish to have disclosed, you also might want to consider having employees sign an NDA.

Provisions of a typical NDA include:

- **Trade secrets covered by the agreement**, specifying what information is included

- **Purpose of the NDA**, describing what the contractor may use the information for and for how long

- **Nondisclosure**, describing the contractor's promise not to disclose the specified information. This section includes all the ways in which the contractor may not use the information, usually in the form of an agreement.

- **Return of materials**, specifying when materials used by the contractor must be returned

- **Exclusions**, providing that if information because publicly available, for example, the contractor has the right to use such information

- **Effective date**, in which the contractor and client agree to an end date for the agreement (not standard)

- **Warranties and representations**, in which the client declares that the information is its property

- **Injunctive relief**, which describes the rights of the client if the contractor is in violation of the agreement. This section states the client's right to obtain an injunction to prevent the contractor from further disclosures, to prevent further damage from these disclosures. Language also may be included to get the contractor to agree to the fines imposed for continued violation; these are usually prohibitive amounts.

The disclosure of confidential information is a serious offense, and companies have a right to protect themselves from such violations. That is why the NDA is such an important document. As a contractor and employer, you will have many occasions to sign NDAs in the course of your business.

chapter 12

Copyrights, Patents, and Trade Secrets

Regardless of the type of industry you are in, you must have at least a basic understanding of the laws that govern intellectual property. Intellectual property is property that has been created by the mind – such as inventions, original writings, and sound recordings – and that is protected under federal law in the United States.

Failure to abide by the rules regarding intellectual property can have legal consequences. If you plagiarize a piece of written work, for example, the person who holds the copyright can sue you. If you have questions about copyright, patent, or trade secret laws, consult an attorney who specializes in intellectual property.

Copyright Laws

One of the biggest issues, especially for writers and those who create their own work, is copyright. Whether you are a writer or you create some other work that is copyrighted, you should have a basic understanding of copyright law and how it works.

Copyright law only protects certain types of work, including original songs, films, architecture, computer software, novels, poetry, and short stories.

Copyright law does not cover ideas. Say you have an idea for a movie script, and you pitch it to a Hollywood executive. The executive may tell you he is not interested at the time, but he may hire another screenwriter to write the script based on your idea. Unfortunately, you have absolutely no legal recourse. You cannot copyright an idea. In addition to ideas, copyright law does not protect systems, facts, or forms of operation.

According to the U.S. Copyright Office, your work is protected by U.S. copyright law from the moment you create it. Registering a piece of work with the U.S. Copyright Office is not necessary; however, there are numerous reasons to consider registering what you have created.

First, if someone has stolen your work, you must register that work with the U.S. Copyright Office before you file a lawsuit. Second, officially copyrighting your work will protect you in the United States and in those countries that have a copyright agreement with the United States.

To register a work, you must fill out an application and pay the current application fee of $45 per work. It takes about four months for the application to be reviewed.

Poor Man's Copyright

Many people have heard of the "poor man's copyright." The idea is as follows. Mail a written or printed copy of the work to yourself in a sealed envelope. When you receive the envelope, do not open it. The stamp date on the sealed envelope documents when you created the work.

While the poor man's copyright may sound like a good idea, it may not hold up in a court of law. According to the U.S. Copyright Office, "The practice of sending a copy of your own work to yourself is sometimes called a 'poor man's copyright.' There is no provision in the copyright law regarding any such type of protection, and it is not a substitute for registration." You can read more about copyright law at the U.S. Copyright Office's Web page: **www.copyright.gov**.

Always keep the copyright laws in mind, especially when you write your own copy for your Web site or promotional materials. If you hire someone to write for you, ensure that the work is original. With the widespread availability of information on the Internet, plagiarism has become a rampant problem. If you are caught in violation of copyright laws, you can face substantial fines.

Retaining Copyright When Hiring an Independent Contractor

If you hire an independent contractor or freelancer to create a work for you – whether it is brochure content or a Web site – you may want to retain the exclusive copyright to that work. That means the independent contractor who created the work has no rights to the work, and he or she will be unable to use it in his or her portfolio or as a sample of work without your written consent.

To ensure that the independent contractor understands and agrees to transferring exclusive copyright to you, have a contract that states the terms of the agreement. A professional will not give you exclusive copyright until you have paid for the project in full. Holding copyright until full payment is received is one way for independent contractors to protect themselves against unscrupulous clients who have no intention of paying for the completed work.

Copyright Problems

As was noted above, there is a growing problem on the Internet concerning copyright infringements. Even if you state you own the copyright of a particular product – an e-book, an article, or even your Web site's content

– you risk having it stolen. The Internet is a vast, open space, making it easy for people to lift other people's work and publish it as their own.

To discover if your work published online has been stolen, you can use Copyscape, a popular online resource that allows you to determine if your work is being used without your permission. Go to **www.copyscape.com** and type in the URL where your work resides. After you hit the "submit" button, Copyscape will scan the Internet in search of your content. It often takes just a few minutes to run the scan.

If your work has been stolen and is being used by another business or individual online, you have several avenues of recourse. Contact the Webmaster of the site that is displaying the stolen work. The Webmaster should remove the content from his or her site immediately. If the Webmaster does not remove the stolen material, contact the Internet service provider who hosts the Web site. Internet service providers frown upon the infringement of copyright laws and will shut down a Web site that has stolen content.

Patents

Patents are a way for inventors to claim ownership to their inventions. As with copyrights, some inventions can and others cannot be patented.

The United States Patent and Trademark Office is responsible for issuing patents. According to the USPTO, inventors can patent:

- A process

- A machine

- An article of manufacture

- A composition of matter

- Business systems

Additionally, an improvement on any of the above can be patented.

On the other hand, you cannot patent:

- Abstract ideas

- Physical phenomena

- Literary works

- Dramatic works

- Musical works

- Artistic works

- Laws of nature

- Those products that are deemed morally offensive

- Those products that are not useful

Consider whether or not you want to apply for a patent. Understand that the application process is long and expensive and can be difficult. If you have invented a product and shared it publicly, however, you may want to file for a patent.

According to the United States' patent laws, you have only one year to apply for a patent once you have sold your invention, talked about it in a publication, or presented it at a trade show. Should you fail to file for a patent during that year, you only have two options. You can either give up your right to apply for a patent for your invention, or you can apply for a provisional patent. A provisional patent allows you another full year so you can raise the money to pay for the patent.

Rather than going through the process of applying for a patent on your own, your best bet is to hire an attorney who specializes in patents to help you through the process.

If you have invented a system, there are two avenues you can take. You can apply for the patent, or you can offer other businesses the opportunity to use the system if they apply for and pay for a license. If you decide to offer a license to your system, make sure you have an attorney write a contract that details the terms, including the length and cost of the license.

To learn more about the patent process, visit the USPTO's Web site at **www.uspto.gov**.

chapter 13

Using the Law

Finding an Attorney

In the course of your business, you will find there are many circumstances that require the services of an attorney. Here are a few of the possibilities:

- You are asked to sign a lease for an office building.

- A recently fired employee is threatening to sue you for discrimination.

- You want to be sure of your rights in a client agreement.

- You have received a notice of suit by a person who claims that you used his name in your advertising without his permission.

- You want to buy a building for your expending business.

- You want to trademark your business name and logo.

In all these situations and more, you should have an attorney. It is important to note that attorneys have different specialties. As the examples above illustrate, you may require the services of a real estate attorney, an employment attorney, a contract attorney, or a general business attorney.

Finding someone who is an expert in all areas of business law is difficult. When you are considering an attorney, look for a small law firm that has individuals with these specializations. There may be one attorney in the group whom you use for most of your general business work, but it can be helpful to have others you and your primary attorney can use for special projects. For example, if you have a copyright issue, you can turn to the copyright expert. Using a group saves you time and effort in trying to find experts in various fields.

Using the Services of an Attorney

Attorneys charge varying rates depending on the market, their experience and specialization, and the type of client. Most attorneys charge upwards of $200 an hour in a medium-size city, while attorneys in larger cities may charge more.

A good attorney can be a valuable asset for your business, but it is important to know when to call and when not to call your lawyer.

If you are presented with a contract that you have never seen before, ask your attorney to review it but not to rewrite any portion of the contract without your express permission. Your attorney may love to write, but consider the hourly rates: The cost of a simple rewrite can be quite high. If you are not comfortable rewriting a contract yourself, you may decide to have your attorney do it; however, you also have the option of going back to the other party and asking that the sections in question be rewritten.

If you need advice on employee matters, you should be comfortable enough with your attorney to be able to discuss these issues. When you are hiring your first employee, discuss various issues; for example, what should you do in common crisis situations, such as when an employee is threatening people? Having a general idea of what you can and cannot do will save you from trying to find your attorney in an emergency.

If you are contemplating legal action or firing someone, call your attorney and discuss the matter. You may have other options, and your attorney can advise you if you do not have enough information or documentation to proceed with the lawsuit.

At the beginning of your business, your attorney can help you set up specific types of forms and agreements that you will use on a regular basis. Then you will not have to keep going back to the attorney each time a situation presents itself.

Establish a good relationship with your attorney at the start of your business. Discussing possible situations with the attorney will give you confidence about taking legal action and avoiding lawsuits in the future.

Legal Research

Before calling your attorney and spending your money, consider using the Internet or your local library for legal research. The IRS, for example, has an excellent Web site, including a great deal of information for small-business owners. You can read documents and print them out for review, and many of your business tax questions can be answered online.

Another good source of legal information online is the Small Business Administration. Its Web site, at **www.sba.gov**, has links to many legal sites that can help with specific questions.

Other legal sites can be accessed through a search engine, such as Google. Although it may take a little longer, finding the legal information you need on your own can save you money.

chapter 14

Retirement Options for the Self-Employed

Most people do not want to spend the rest of their life working. While you may always want to work in some form or another, it is important to make sure you will be comfortable in your retirement years. It is not too soon to start thinking about a retirement plan for yourself and your employees.

Planning for Retirement

There are two basic plan types: defined benefit and defined contribution. Defined benefit plans were used primarily by most companies until a few years ago. In this type of plan, the company assures the employee of a specific benefit amount for the rest of his or her life, depending on options chosen. This type of plan is subject to more regulation and is very costly to the employer.

Many companies have started changing to defined contribution plans, in which the company, and often the employee, contributes specified amounts to an account. After the employee is vested (i.e., has full rights to the benefit), he or she can manage the investments in the plan. A fully vested employee can take the account with him or her when leaving the company, even if he or she is not retiring.

Types of Retirement Plans for Businesses

Here are some of the options:

1. Individual retirement account. You can contribute a specified amount each year to an IRA, depending on whether or not you have a pension plan in place with another employer.

2. SEP-IRA. Sometimes confused with an IRA, a SEP-IRA allows an employer to set up a separate IRA account for each employee, to be managed by the individual employee. The employer may contribute to the plan, up to 25 percent of the employee's income, to a maximum amount each year. The employee also may contribute to this plan.

3. Keogh plan. This is a full-fledged retirement plan and not an individual retirement account. There are many options to this type of plan, and if you are considering one, you should check with a financial planner for details.

4. 401(k) plans are defined contribution plans that provide for employer contributions based on employee income. These plans, like IRAs, give employees the right to manage their investment and to take the account with them when they leave, if they are fully vested in the plan.

5. Stocks. Many companies give employees the option to purchase company stock, sometimes at a reduced price or for lower or no investment fees. If you have a corporation with stock, offering stock to employees is a good way to provide incentive.

Providing Your Employees With Options for Saving for Retirement

If you have employees, you may want to include them in some or all of your benefit and retirement plans. Be aware that federal law requires equal treatment of employees in these plans, depending on classes of employees. This is a complex issue, and you should retain the services of a benefits specialist before you venture into this area.

chapter 15

Hiring/Training/ Motivating/Firing Employees

As a business owner, one of the most difficult and costly decisions you will make is whether to hire employees. If you are working as a service professional, you may not need any employees, but you may need to hire independent contractors to work for you. If you are producing and/or selling a product, you may have to hire employees to help with the workload. Before you decide to hire an employee or an independent contractor, consider the benefits and drawbacks of each relationship.

Benefits Versus Drawbacks of Employees

The most obvious benefit to employees is their ability to help you with all the work of running the business. Employees can:

- Greet customers and help new customers

- Collect money

- Help customers with complaints and problems

- Provide extra services that supplement your main services

- Display, stock, ship, and sell products

- Do bookkeeping and other administrative tasks

- Help with general marketing and advertising duties

- Assist with special promotions and events

- Do all the little tasks you do not want to do

Be aware of the disadvantages to hiring employees. If you have employees, you must do the following:

- Hire in an ethical manner, without bias or discrimination

- Provide a reasonable amount of pay, depending on the level of work each employee performs

- Collect and pay payroll taxes, including FICA (Social Security) and Medicare, federal and state unemployment, and workers' compensation on the amounts of your payroll

- Deal with employee interpersonal problems and issues. Even if you have only one employee, this person can cause problems that can take time to solve

- Deal with employee theft and dishonesty

- Pay benefits, such as health insurance

- Pay for unproductive time, including holidays, vacations, sick leave, and personal time

- Hire new employees to replace those who leave or are dismissed

Most small-business owners have reservations about hiring employees, not only because they must be paid but thanks to the many issues mentioned before. However, the benefits should not be ignored. A good employee can be a great asset to a business, particularly in the area of customer service. If your customers come to like your employees, they feel more connected to your business and are more eager to return. It is impossible for you to be everywhere and do everything, particularly as your business grows. Hiring other people to help with customer service and administrative duties allows you to focus on other things you need to do as a professional and gives you more time to grow your business.

Hiring Independent Contractors

Before you decide to hire your first employee, think about the benefits of hiring an independent contractor instead. This may be beneficial in two particular instances: an assistant and a bookkeeper.

Hiring a Virtual Assistant

Hiring an assistant or a virtual assistant can give you the benefits of having an employee without any drawbacks. In the example of a virtual assistant, or online assistant, you hire the person on a monthly basis at an hourly rate. Most virtual assistants require a minimum number of hours per month as a retainer, so you need to have enough work to keep them busy each month. As you are hiring them as an independent contractor, you do not need to pay payroll taxes or benefits. If the relationship does not work out, you can terminate it at any time. VAs are trained at their jobs, and many are bonded, so you have some protection against theft and dishonesty.

VAs are highly experienced business specialists who work from home or from their own offices, have their own equipment, and provide various services to business owners.

If you think you need help to get things done correctly and on time, you are most likely right. However, you may not want to deal with a person who is on site, who has only basic skills, who requires a salary, and who requires insurance, taxes, and vacation and sick leave. If that is the case, a VA may be perfect for you.

CASE STUDY: CINDY GAFFEN

Cindy Gaffen is the owner of Virtually Fantastic, a virtual assisting business. She has owned this company for three years. Gaffen enjoys the freedom of being self-employed and, above all, the ability to manage her own business. In the beginning, her biggest challenge was securing her first client, but once she started, she was profitable in about four months.

She learned the hard way not to take on less-than-ideal clients and to be persistent. She relied on family and friends, the SBA, and AssistU, a VA training organization. Her advice to you is, "Figure out what you want to do and do it! Being self-employed is hard work and time consuming, but it is more fulfilling, challenging, and exhilarating than any job."

cindy@virtuallyfantastic.com / Phone: 1-847-231-3972

Costs of Hiring Employees

Employees can be an expensive proposition for a small business. Required payroll taxes and additional benefits can increase your payroll costs between 20 and 30 percent above the wage rate you are paying each employee. For the average small-business owner, these costs can be very high. Consider the following examples:

- **Social Security and Medicare.** For each employee, you are required to pay 7.65 percent of his or her gross pay for Social Security and Medicare. You must pay these amounts to the IRS, along with the amounts you have withheld from employees for federal and state income tax, on a monthly or quarterly basis, depending on the size of your payroll. For an employer paying $10 an hour to an employee, this is an extra $0.765 for each hour worked.

- **Unemployment compensation.** For each payroll, you are required to make a payment into a fund that provides unemployment benefits to workers who are terminated (except under egregious circumstances). The effective federal unemployment compensation tax rate is 0.8 percent gross tax on the first $7,000 of pay annually. Although this may not look like a lot at first glance, this tax can add up if you have several employees. Most states also have an unemployment compensation program into which you might have to pay.

- **Workers' compensation.** You also must pay into a federal and probably a state fund to provide benefits to workers who are injured on the job. The rates for this tax vary based on the type of employer and the number of injuries and illnesses incurred by employees. For example, coal mine operators pay a higher amount for workers' compensation than employers of office employees.

Employee Health and Safety

The provisions of the Occupational Safety and Health Act (OSHA) of 1974 impose a number of requirements on you as an employer, even if you have only one employee. The purpose of OSHA regulations is to provide employees a safe work environment and to minimize their risk of on-the-job illness or injury. The provisions of OSHA include these requirements:

- You must allow OSHA inspectors to visit your office, unannounced, either in response to an employee complaint or just to check on your business.

- You must have an OSHA-compliant poster on display where employees can see it, explaining the provisions of OSHA and their rights under this law.

- You must be sure that all hazardous substances with which employees come in contact are properly labeled and that material safety data sheets are available to help employees know what to do in the case of an accident involving one of these substances. Note that hazardous substances can be household cleaning supplies, if they are used in quantities greater than used in the average home.

- Employees working in health care offices must be provided with equipment and personal protection in case of exposure to blood-borne pathogens (blood and body fluids) to protect them against exposure to HIV/AIDS and Hepatitis B.

You must provide employees with the following training:

- Handling hazardous substances, such as workplace chemicals

- Dealing with blood-borne pathogens using universal precautions in health care offices.

- You must have procedures for dealing with fires and other emergencies, in order to respond properly and allow employees to safely exit the building.

- You must keep accurate records of workplace-related illnesses, accidents, and injuries.

These precautions are required and need to be implemented when you hire your first employee.

You also should train employees about what to do if an OSHA inspector comes to your office or workplace. Many small-business owners create an OSHA manual, train employees on it when they are hired, and continue training on a yearly basis.

Types of Employees

Employees are classified according to the duties they perform and the level of experience and education their job requires. The purpose of this classification is to determine whether the business owner is required to pay an employee overtime. Employees can be classified as either "exempt" or "non-exempt."

The Federal Wage and Hour Laws, determined by the Fair Labor Standards Act (FLSA), require employers to pay non-exempt employees overtime over 40 hours a week. If you permit an employee to work more than 40 hours in any one week, you must pay overtime at time and a half. Overtime is required to be paid even if the person did not work 40 hours during the previous week. For example, if you have an employee who worked 45 hours in one week and 35 hours in the second week, you may not carry over the extra five hours from the first week to the second week. To ensure that employers are in compliance with this law, the Wage and Hour division requires that employers keep track of employee time with time cards or time sheets and that these documents be signed each week by both employer and employee.

Exempt employees, on the other hand, are excluded from overtime pay. An employee is exempt if he or she is professional, supervisory, or managerial. For example, a teacher is a professional, thus exempt from being paid overtime, as is an office manager or a factory supervisor. For the protection of employees, the FLSA assumes that overtime should be paid, unless the employer can provide evidence that the position is exempt. Notice that it is not the person who is considered exempt but the position. This is another reason to detail the job duties, education, and experience requirements: If you label an employee "exempt," you can show your justification. You have to prove that a professional level of education and experience is required for this position.

Hiring Your First Employee

If you are starting your business and decide you need to hire an employee, the first thing you need to do is determine the requirements of the position, in terms of duties, education, training, and experience. The clearer you are about these requirements, the easier it will be for you to find the right person for the position.

Begin your hiring plan with a checklist, considering both the job itself and the needs of your business. Answer the following questions:

- What specific tasks will be involved with this job?

- What skills will be needed in order to perform these tasks?

- What experience will be required in order to have these skills?

- Will a certain level of education be required?

- What personal characteristics will this person need? Will he or she deal with people in a customer service capacity, or will the job require attention to detail, as in bookkeeping or billing?

- What physical requirements will be needed? Will this person have to stand for long periods of time? Will he or she need to lift heavy objects (specify how heavy these objects might be)? Will the person need to drive?

- What kinds of machines or equipment will the person need to operate?

- What amount of pay will you provide? Will the person be paid weekly? Monthly? Hourly?

- Will this position be classified as exempt or non-exempt?

- What are the hours for this position? What days will the person be required to work? Is weekend or evening work required?

- What benefits will you provide?

Recruiting Employees

After you decide on the duties and requirements of the position to be filled, start the recruiting process. Most small-business owners begin by placing an advertisement in a local newspaper. Make your ad as specific as possible to be sure you attract the right applicants for the position. If you are not specific, you will have many unqualified people applying for the job, and you will have to wade through many applications to find ones that are suitable.

For example, an advertisement stating, "Front desk receptionist. Friendly and smiling. High school education, no previous experience" is going to ensure that you will have many applications to look at. On the other hand, consider this ad: "Front desk receptionist needed for busy office. Must have minimum two years of experience in receptionist position. Some college required. Associate degree in business preferred. Friendly attitude a must." While you still may receive many applications, you can weed out the most obvious misfits quickly.

Many employers today ask for an e-mail application to make the process more efficient and to check that candidates can deal with e-mail attachments. It is also possible that, depending on the type of position, you may want applications to be mailed to see if applicants can follow directions. Those that do not comply with your requirements (asking for references with the application, for example) should be eliminated immediately.

In considering that stack of applications, remember that you are only hiring one person. Your task is to find no more than five or six top applicants to interview. Set aside the non-qualified applicants and make a pile of the applications that might be possibilities, keeping up to a dozen of the most promising.

Then make phone calls, paying particular attention to the tone of voice of the person. If you are hiring for a customer service position, like the aforementioned receptionist, listen to hear if the person has a smile. Even if you cannot see him or her, you can tell by a voice whether this person is smiling, interested, and generally pleasant. Ask a few questions about availability and interest in the position. Be sure to include a question about salary requirements. If the person hesitates or states a minimum salary that is higher than you are willing to pay, thank the person and move on.

The purpose of the phone interview is to help you select the top five or six people to invite into your office for an interview. In planning the office interview process, consider the following:

- If you have other employees, invite them to participate in the interview process. Seeing how well the new person gets along with current employees can be an important factor in your hiring decision. If the current employees express concern about an applicant, listen to them. Having several people provide input on an applicant gives you more information on which to base your hiring decision.

- Include some time for each applicant to work in your office for a few hours to see how well the person understands and complies with your office processes. You also can see if a person is uncomfortable with the main duties of the position.

- Allow time for the applicant's questions. If an applicant does not have many questions, it may be that you have answered them, or it could be that the person is not really interested. If most of the questions relate to pay and benefits, question the person's motives in applying for the position.

- Consider including tests in the interview process. Some small-business owners include an intelligence test or a typing or math test if this is important to the position. You can test applicants as long as you test all and not just some of them.

- Require all applicants to fill out an application form during the interview process. Ask for at least three references from each applicant, at least one of which must be a former employer, if possible. Encourage professional references rather than neighbors and friends. Let each applicant know you will be checking references.

Interviewing Applicants

Spend time interviewing each applicant one-on-one. During the interview, ask open questions that cause the applicant to think and give undirected responses. For example, do not ask, "How long did you work at your previous employer?" The answer will be short and will not give you much information. Instead ask, "What parts of your last job did you like the most, what did you like the least, and why?"

Structure the interview as follows:

- Begin with a general question that the person can answer easily, to get him or her more comfortable.

- Include several "what would you do in this situation" questions. These are called behavioral questions, and they provide you with a great deal of information on how the person deals with situations. These questions should be directly related to the duties of the position. For example, in the case of a receptionist, ask how he or she has dealt with irate people on the phone or how the applicant would deal with that situation.

- Include direct questions about the person's education and experience. If there are gaps or answers that are incomplete, do not be afraid to probe. You have a right to know if this person is lying or leaving out information that may be negative.

- Leave the specifics of the position to the end of the interview. If you discuss the job first, the applicant will be primed to answer in the way he or she thinks you want, rather than giving you more sincere answers. For example, if you state at the beginning of the interview that you want him or her to handle multiple tasks (phone calls and visitors) at the same time, you most certainly will hear the applicant talk about how he or she can handle phone calls and visitors at the same time. Listen first to what the applicant says and see if it fits what you are looking for, rather than having the applicant tell you what you want to hear.

Avoiding Bias in Interviewing and Hiring

One of the most common mistakes made by business owners new to the hiring process is to introduce elements of bias and discrimination. In most cases, this is unintended, but even unintentional discrimination can cause you problems. It is important to keep bias out of your interviewing and hiring process.

Check your employment application form to be sure it does not include information that might reveal unnecessary information that might be cause for a biased or discriminatory rejection. Here are some guidelines for application forms:

- **You may not ask an applicant's age.** It is not appropriate or necessary to ask an applicant's age. You may ask if he or she is above 18, if that is the age of majority in your state.

- **You may not ask about arrest records.** You may ask only about convictions and the subject of the conviction.

- **You may not ask about height or weight**, unless these are requirements of the position. For example, some airlines have height and weight restrictions for flight attendants.

- **You may not ask the applicant's country of origin, citizenship, race, parentage, or nationality.** You may ask if the person is legally able to work in the country, and you may ask the person to provide proof of legal work status after hire.

- **You may not ask about marital status or children.**

- **You may ask if the applicant has been in the military,** but you may not ask about the type of discharge.

- **You may not ask about the national origin of an applicant's name,** but you may ask if the applicant has worked under a different name.

- **You may not ask if an applicant is pregnant.**

In an interview, here are some areas that you should avoid:

- **You may not ask about children or babysitters**, but you may ask if the applicant can meet the job requirements, including overtime, if it may be required.

- **You may not ask about religious affiliations or organizations**, but you may ask about any civic organizations or volunteer work done by the applicant.

- **You may not ask if the applicant speaks other languages**, unless speaking another language is a specific requirement of the job.

In general, consider these two rules of thumb when interviewing and hiring applicants:

1. Everything you ask an applicant and everything you consider about an applicant should be a "bona fide occupational qualification," meaning that it must be directly related to the job duties and qualifications you require for the position. Other questions or requirements that are not related to the job cannot be asked.

2. You can require something of one applicant only if you require it of all applicants (at least those you choose to interview), such as an intelligence test or a typing or bookkeeping test.

What you want to avoid in your interviewing and hiring practices is the appearance of bias and prejudice against an applicant. Treating all job applicants the same way, requiring the same things of all applicants, and avoiding questions that can be considered biased will help you avoid a possible discrimination lawsuit.

Determining Whom to Hire

After you have interviewed several applicants, you may find there is one who stands out and is the best qualified. If no candidate stands out, you have several options:

- Go through your original pile of promising applications and make sure you have not missed someone. This occasionally brings someone to light who might be a good candidate so it is worth another look.

- You can reject all the applicants and start over with a new application, interview, and hiring process. Most business owners choose not to do this, because they need someone immediately and want to make a decision and have the job filled.

You can re-interview the top applicants, looking at the job description more carefully and considering other factors that you might not have emphasized before. In many cases, a re-appraisal of the top applicants brings to light new qualities.

Rejecting Applicants

Expect to have many applicants who will not be hired. For those who came in for an interview, take the time to call each one personally. You should not be specific about why this person was not hired; in fact, it is better if you do not go into details. Just say politely but firmly, "Another applicant was chosen for the position. Thank you for your time." Going into detail about why an applicant was not chosen can lead that person to question your process and also may lead to charges of bias. The more general you can be, the better.

For applicants who were not interviewed, send each one a letter as soon as possible. In the letter, be as general as possible about the reason for not hiring the person, stating, "Another more suitable applicant was chosen for the position." If a rejected applicant calls you and you cannot avoid talking with him or her, just repeat your words from your letter and tell the person politely but firmly that you cannot talk about the situation anymore.

New Employee Probationary Period

When you make a job offer to an applicant, talk with him or her about the general job duties and expectations, discuss the starting date, and explain the starting salary. You also should explain that there is a probationary period for the job. The purpose of probation is for both your company and the new employee to see if there is a good fit between the person and the job and the company. At any time during probation, the employee may leave or the company may ask the employee to leave, in either case without notice.

Emphasize that the probationary period, usually 90 days or three months, is not a guarantee of a job for that time. It may be necessary to terminate someone for a major fault or dishonesty, and you do not want to have to keep him or her for 90 days.

It is best not to put a hire offer in writing for non-exempt employees. When you are hiring a person for an executive or professional position, however, you may need an employment contract. This document should be prepared by your company's attorney to be sure that both parties are protected.

Tips for Training Employees

New employee training should be a well-thought-out process beginning with the first day on the job and continuing for several weeks. Training new employees ensures that your expectations for their performance matches their understanding of what is expected of them. The more thoroughly you train an employee, the greater your assurance that this person will be a productive and happy part of your company.

The first day on the job should be spent watching and listening. Explain the general company policies and the benefits provided by the company. If you have an office policy manual, have the new employee sign that document.

If the new employee is replacing someone and the person who is leaving the job is available, have that person conduct the training. If this is not possible, find another employee to do this or do the training yourself. Follow these principles of education in setting up your training program:

- First, tell what needs to be done. Create specific task sequences for the new person, so he or she can understand what has to be done. Walk through the list with the new employee. If you want the person to answer the phone with a certain phrase, for example, have the phrase available on a card by the phone.

- Then, show the person how the job is to be done. Demonstrate the duties, talking through each one. For the phone answering phrase, for example, answer the phone yourself, using the tone of voice you prefer.

- Next, have the person do the task. Listen and watch while the person answers the phone. Provide feedback and praise when the job is done correctly.

- Finally, follow up during the training period to make sure that each task is done correctly and provide feedback as necessary. In the case of a new receptionist, periodically stop and listen to him or her answer the phone; if you observe any problems, point out and explain them.

In addition, allow time for other people who will be working with the new employee to spend time with him or her to explain their jobs and how they relate to the job duties of the new employee.

Evaluating Employee Performance

Even during the training period, a new employee's performance should be evaluated. You want to be aware of potential problems as soon as possible.

The new employee's supervisor should keep notes on the person's performance, including both positive and negative incidents. Toward the end of the probationary period, the supervisor should have a formal discussion with the employee about his or her performance. If there are obvious and significant problems with the employee's performance, do not wait until the end of the probationary period to terminate him or her. Tell the employee, "This employment relationship is not working out. We are terminating you effective immediately." Although you do not have to pay any severance pay, you can do this if you want.

If the employee survives the probationary period, the supervisor should continue to maintain notes on the employee's performance. A formal performance review should be conducted with each employee at least every six months. During the performance review, strengths should be noted, as well as areas that need improvement. Some companies include a discussion of goals, asking the employee to set goals for the next six months and then evaluating progress toward those goals at the next performance review.

It is important to conduct regular review and evaluation sessions with each employee. The purpose of these reviews is to let employees know what job duties they are performing satisfactorily and in what areas they need to improve. Your purpose in these reviews is to recognize employees who are doing well and to inform employees who are not doing well that they need to improve. Your job is to make your expectations clear and to warn unsatisfactory employees that their failure to improve could lead to termination.

Terminating Employees

One of the business owner's most difficult tasks is firing employees. Employees may be fired for several reasons:

- **Incompetence:** failure to perform job duties satisfactorily

- **Behavior:** e.g., missing work, tardiness, or dress code violations

- **Dishonesty and illegal behavior:** stealing, using drugs at work, or harassing customers or other employees

Firing an employee for dishonesty or illegal behavior should be done immediately after the behavior is discovered. Before you terminate for such behavior, call your company attorney and explain the situation. Follow your attorney's advice. In some cases, such as theft or embezzlement, you may need to call the police before you do anything else.

If the employee's behavior is threatening to others, as in the case of drunkenness, or the employee is harassing others, remove the person from the situation first and then call your attorney.

Attendance problems are the most common reason for firings, but they are also the most difficult to deal with. Here is one suggested process for dealing with this problem:

1. From the first day, provide each employee with a written statement of your expectations regarding attendance and tardiness. Explain what tardiness means (five minutes late? 15 minutes late?). State how the employee should notify you of lateness or absence. Explain how attendance is documented (on an attendance sheet or a time card) and include a statement that forgery of the time document is cause for dismissal.

2. Keep written documentation of each employee's attendance and tardiness in addition to the time sheet.

3. If an employee shows signs of being tardy on a regular basis, have a discussion with him or her about the expectations you laid out at hiring. Explain that if the problem continues, it could be cause for dismissal. This is usually a difficult discussion, because people who are tardy often have many excuses and sometimes legitimate personal or family issues. Express sympathy and state that you still require attendance and punctuality of every employee. Repeat again that continued absence and tardiness could result in termination.

4. If the absences or tardiness continue, do not hesitate to terminate the employee. Be sure you have documentation of all these absences. Also be certain that you are not treating this employee differently from others. If you allow another employee to be absent or late and you do not discipline him or her in the same way as the person you are terminating, you are leaving yourself and your company open to charges of discrimination. Following the same process with every employee will leave you in a good position to fight a discrimination charge.

Terminating an employee for incompetence also requires the same procedure. Incompetence may become evident during the probationary period. Do not hesitate to terminate an incompetent employee during probation.

Problems with employee performance may not show up until after the probationary period. In this case, the six-month review may be the best time to discuss them. Make certain that you document problems and give the employee the opportunity to do better; this is the time for goal setting, as discussed above. If the employee has been given an adequate number of opportunities to improve and has not done anything to make these improvements, you may consider termination. The termination discussion, when it comes, should not be a surprise to the employee.

To conduct the termination discussion, consider having another employee or someone you trust as a witness to the discussion. Keep the meeting short, and do it at the end of the day, at the beginning of a work week. Having the discussion at the beginning of the week gives the employee time to start looking for another job immediately, rather than spending the weekend worrying and being upset. Begin the discussion by explaining that you have given the person an adequate number of attempts to improve and that he or she has not resolved the performance issues. State that you are terminating him or her effective immediately.

Give the employee a letter explaining the reasons for the termination. Be as specific as possible, including a listing of the times you have counseled the person, the things that you requested be improved, and the failure to improve. During the discussion, talk about any severance pay due to the employee and any benefits that are being stopped, and let the person know when the final paycheck will be received.

After the discussion, escort the person to his or her desk and monitor while the desk and personal belongings are cleared out. The employee can use the computer to gather up personal e-mail or other personal files that can be put onto a USB drive or another external storage device. Verify which files are being taken off the computer. Look through any papers or documents the employee wishes to take, as well as any personal belongings, to make sure there is nothing that belongs to your company that you do not want taken from the office. Finally, escort the person to the door and watch as he or she leaves.

If the employee wants to complain or cause a problem, your witness or someone else might be needed to escort the person out of the office. This is one of the main reasons for having someone else with you to help with this process. If you suspect that the person might become agitated or violent, do not hesitate to call the local police for assistance.

In a small business, employee problems occur more frequently than you might expect. The process of terminating an employee is difficult. However, if you document the situation and keep the exit process brief and to the point, you can avoid problems.

How to Motivate Your Employees

Dealing with good employees who work diligently to help your business succeed is one of the best parts of having a small business. Enthusiastic, competent, and trustworthy team members can be a major element in the success of your business. Your biggest concern with good employees is how to keep them motivated and interested in staying with your company.

In a small business, there are not many opportunities for promotion, and you cannot afford to give large pay increases. Yet, there are several ways of keeping good employees motivated:

1. Consider individual employee needs when determining benefits. Time off, for example, can be given to employees on an individual basis. You might find that one employee appreciates flexible hours, while another prefers working more hours four days a week and taking one day off. As long as the 40-hour rule is followed and customer service and business needs are being met, you can give each employee a work schedule that appeals to the person.

2. If your business structure allows, consider allowing exempt employees to work from home for part of their work hours. Non-exempt employees should not work from home, because their hours must be tracked for overtime purposes.

3. Provide incentives to employees for participating in the success of your business. Set up both long-term and short-term incentives. For example, give team bonuses for meeting monthly production or sales goals. Set up a major annual goal and make the associated incentive something that all employees can enjoy together. If you have a small office, take all employees for a fun weekend somewhere. If your office is larger, a dinner celebration might be good.

4. Provide employees the opportunity for personal and professional growth and development. Allow each employee to take a course or seminar each year to improve work skills. Take the employees as a group to a motivational seminar. Have a speaker come to your business to educate employees.

5. Provide fun and low-cost benefits based on requests from employees. Prepare a list of possible benefits and ask employees which they would prefer. Be creative or ask employees for suggestions. Some examples are free coffee each morning; weekly yoga, stress relief, or meditation classes; membership to a fitness center; and tickets to sporting events or concerts. Choose the most popular according to your budget. As a note, most benefits can be considered legitimate business expenses and may be deductible as expenses on your income tax. Check with your tax advisor on the deductibility of these benefits.

6. Allow employees to participate in the company's operational decisions. Have a weekly or monthly meeting of all employees. Make these sessions as positive as possible. Include recognition of employees and teams who have reached goals and discuss company highlights and growth. Ask for employee suggestions, in written or verbal form. Then discuss how to implement these suggestions. Such meetings are easier to conduct in a small business. In a larger business, have employees hold discussions in separate groups. While you may not be able to implement all the suggestions, at least you

have listened. For many people, being listened to and having their opinions considered is a great motivation.

7. The best motivation for employees is individual recognition. While recognition of team efforts is good, people want to be recognized for their unique efforts. This is why many companies have an "employee of the month" recognition program. You may want to consider instituting such a program or something like it. One way to gather information about employees is to ask customers their opinions. Use customer feedback in employee newsletters or on bulletin boards. Certainly, include a "kudos" section in your employee meetings. Some companies give the "employee of the month" extra rewards, like a special parking place or a free dinner at a local restaurant.

Encouraging teamwork, providing special benefits, and recognizing individual efforts will help maintain motivation, loyalty, and productivity.

How to Be an Effective Boss

It is easy for many people to describe an ineffective boss but not as easy to describe what makes a boss effective. In a small company, how you treat your employees will be a major factor not only in their decision to stay with you but in their productivity and growth as employees. Here are three recognized traits of an effective boss:

1. Treat employees with fairness. This may be difficult, because fairness is often a matter of perception. What seems fair to one person may not seem fair to another. Over time, your attempts at fairness should be recognized by employees. For example, your ability to meet employees' individual needs for time off will be seen as equitable.

2. Consider each employee as an individual. This does not conflict with being fair; on the contrary, it is a complementary aspect of being an

effective employer. Demonstrate recognition for individual efforts and, more importantly, listen to employees' concerns and take them seriously.

3. Be an enthusiastic leader. People follow a leader who knows where he or she is going and who provides followers with his or her vision. Sharing your vision with your employees and helping them grow with the company are the best ways to be a leader.

resources r

1. The Directory of Associations: **http://www.marketingsource.com/associations/information.html**

2. For information on state workers' compensation insurance, go to this Web site, which lists laws by state: **http://www.workerscompensationinsurance.com/**.

3. Use this Web site to investigate possible Internet fraud: **http://www.fraud.org/internet/inttip/inttip.htm**.

4. The SBA Web site (**www.sba.gov**) has many resources and information for small-business people.

5. The IRS (**www.irs.gov**) has information on taxes for all kinds of businesses and can help you make decisions on legal forms of practice.

6. For demographic information for your marketing plan, look at these sites:

   a. City-Data: **www.city-data.com**

   b. Ersys (a relocation site covering many cities): **www.ersys.com**

7. **About.com** has many good resources for small businesses: **http://sbinformation.about.com/**.

8. Some other sites with information for small businesses:

a. Idea Café: **www.businessownersideacafe.com/**

b. AllBusiness: **www.allbusiness.com/**

c. Business Know How: **www.businessknowhow.com/**

d. Solo-E: **http://solo-e.com/**

Author
Biography

Dr. Jean Murray

Dr. Jean Murray has been assisting small-business owners with startup and operations for over 27 years. She is also a freelance business writer, with several books to her credit, including *Planning for Practice Success* and *Planning for Writing Success*. Dr. Murray has an M.B.A. and a Ph.D. in business management with an emphasis on entrepreneurship. She began consulting with small-business owners in 1974, and she has owned two successful businesses. Her passion is helping entrepreneurs start and succeed in business.

E-mail Dr. Murray at **jean@thethrivingwriter.com**

P4PS
Planning for Practice Success

Beth Williams

Beth Williams is a full-time writer from Lexington, Virginia. In addition to a B.A. in Journalism and Communications from Point Park University, Beth holds a M.A. in Holocaust and Genocide Studies from The Richard Stockton College of New Jersey.

She is the founder and co-owner of Creative Inklings LC, a full-service writing firm that caters to both online and offline clients and can be found on the Web at **www.creativeinklings.org**. Beth has written hundreds of articles, e-books, audio scripts, reports, and other content for clients on dozens of topics ranging from business to travel. Additionally, she has written for several magazines, including those focusing on business.

Beth is currently taking her extensive writing credentials in a new direction, branching into internet marketing, offering private label rights (PLR) content for marketers, Webmasters, and other clients.

index i